To Lydia

all the Best

The Simple Game

An Irish Jockey's Memoir

The Simple Game

An Irish Jockey's Memoir

Thomas Foley

With a Foreword
by Otto Thorwarth

A Caballo Press of Ann Arbor Book
Ann Arbor, Michigan

*Dedicated to Mam, Dad,
and my Little Boys*

Foreword

The first time I became aware of Tom was in 2009 at Kentucky Downs, a European-style race track located on the border between Kentucky and Tennessee, near the city of Franklin and just off Interstate 65. The course is unique among American tracks in that its surface is grass and not dirt, and instead of the traditional oval shape associated with American tracks, the course resembles a lightbulb lying on its side.

Although I am not a fan of riding at Kentucky Downs, Tom seemed to be in his element, an advantage probably stemming from his days as a steeplechase jockey and the fact that most, if not all, steeplechase races are run on grass.

Tom and I actually met a year later while waiting for our turn to audition for Walt Disney Studios' feature film *Secretariat*. We exchanged stories about our careers, but mostly we shared some laughs over our lack of acting ability.

As fate would have it, I landed the role of Ron Turcotte, Secretariat's first-call jockey, and a month into filming, I discovered that Tom was cast as Jimmy Gaffney, Secretariat's exercise rider. We had a chance to congratulate each other while in Louisiana where we were shooting some of the scenes for the film.

Rain delays during the shoot allowed Tom and me to visit for hours on end. On most days, we traded war stories about our riding careers, as well as a few pertaining to our personal lives, but on one particular night, we decided to try out the cuisine at a local karaoke club. I thought that my primary reason for coming along was to enjoy a good meal and to lend moral support for those brave enough to get up on the stage, but, as I found out later, Tom had other plans.

We had a great time, but by the end of the evening, Tom said he wasn't leaving until I sang at least one song. I did, and I think that was the most nervous I got during the entire filming of the movie.

After my singing debut, if I can call it that, my friendship with Tom grew. We continued talking and then one day he told me about his book. I asked him to send me a copy of the manuscript when it was finished.

He did, and from the first page on, I felt as if we were back in Louisiana talking to each other face-to-face. I was taken by Tom's ability to make me feel this way and felt that a lot of his stories could have been my own by just changing a few names here and there.

As I read through the manuscript, I easily related to the fact that we all struggle to find love, to form strong and lasting relationships, and to find our place in this world. I also connected with the idea that understanding ourselves is a never-ending process.

What struck me most was the frankness with which Tom shared his story. Most people seem to think that the life of a jockey is all glamour and glitz, but as Tom clearly shows it is anything but that.

The psychological impact that the "Sport of Kings" has on the minds of pint-sized athletes are numerous. Jockeys are expected to meet weight limits and to ride horses that they sometimes know have no business on a track, and they are given little credit when they win and all the blame when they don't. Jockeys are also required to spend long hours away from those they love; which often means that they miss opportunities to build solid relationships.

Even so, most jockeys are willing to sacrifice all to become the best in the business.

In horse racing, as in all professional sports, you will find that driven attitude to win and to be the best at the highest level. The sad part is that probably less than five percent of jockeys ever experience that kind of success. Some never reach the top because they lack the talent or made bad career decisions. Then there's those that just never get a break.

After the reality of never reaching the pinnacle of the sport sets in, jockeys have three choices; they can leave the sport, find another job related to the business, or they can fall into the routine of an adrenaline driven grind of being an overworked and underappreciated jockey.

Tom's story is unique in that he came from Ireland as a boy and in time enjoyed tremendous success as a steeplechase jockey. It was only after experiencing personal problems that he selected to ride on flat tracks. At this point in his career, he could've selected to run away from racing altogether, but the crazy part about racing is, that once horse racing gets into your blood, it never really leaves.

There is just something special about the relationship between man and beast working together as one. The relationship is a little like marriage; when you find that special horse, it is like finding your life partner that only you connect with, it becomes a magical partnership that keeps you coming back for more.

As you will discover, there's no doubt that Tom's life was destined to be lived among horses and horse racing and that the sport and horses would play, and continue to play, a huge role in shaping his life. When Tom told me about his book back in Louisiana, I thought that if it was anything like the Tom I was getting to know that it would be something special. I was right.

The Simple Game is one of those books that makes you feel as if the writer is talking to you and that you're forming a friendship with each passing page. As you know, that takes deep-seated honesty, and that is exactly what Tom gives; probably because he doesn't know any other way.

I am proud to call Tom my friend, and know that you will be too.

Enjoy!
Otto Thorwarth
August 2010

*T*he "flipping bowl," every horse race track
in the world has one.

1

Flipping

There were no tears in his eyes.

Tobey Maguire, the actor, raised his head and looked into the mirror. Sure, he had the distressed look on his face, but there were no tears; trust me there's always tears. Maguire was playing the part of jockey Red Pollard in the movie *Seabiscuit* and was purging himself of his latest meal in an attempt to lose weight.

What Maguire was doing is sadly enough my area of expertise and has been a ritual I have performed many times a day for the last few years. I am an expert at the rite of purging so I can tell you that there should've been tears.

Watching Maguire, I felt cheated. I mean, here was a guy getting paid millions to play this part, and I felt for that kind of money he could've at least shed a few tears. Hell, myself and sixty percent of the jockeys riding in this country do it everyday; we do it and brush back the tears just to get our shot at riding a winner or making a decent paycheck.

Our tears are not shed in pain or anguish; our tear ducts tear up in order to clear themselves out as you do this to your body. We call it "flipping" or "heaving," and it runs rampant and unchecked throughout every horse track in the world. The practice is not even frowned upon; it's catered to.

Most jockeys' quarters have a special toilet that is shaped in a square. They're called "flipping bowls". This toilet is solely there for performing the act. Most jocks' room toilets will have four stalls. One through three will have a sign posted inside reading "no flipping in these stalls," yet magic door number four gets all the action.

It's not uncommon to see riders lined up waiting to use it and making jokes about the guy inside who is making ungodly noises. I've made these jokes myself as a way to keep my mind off of what I was going to do when my turn came. The odd thing about it was that we would just stand in line waiting and not use the other toilets. Looking at it now, it's funny when I realize that we even had rules for bulimia.

So how do you become a flipper? For me it was easy. I was at dinner with a few riders, and at the time I was trying to do it right and stick to a diet and use my head. I noticed that most of the other guys were tearing into these huge meals. They didn't seem bothered by the fact that they had to make weight the next day. My curiosity grew to the point that I had to ask, "How can you eat all that and keep your weight in check?"

Big mistake, as the answer I was about to hear would change my whole world and lead me down a road that eventually meant the loss of my passion for racing, a passion I am now trying to desperately rediscover.

"I don't keep it," was the answer.

"What do you mean you don't keep it? What do you do with it?" I asked.

"Easy," my buddy said smiling at me, "I flip."

As with most things in life, one question led to another. "How do you do it?"

This got a few laughs from the five jocks at the table as it's not exactly rocket science, but the answers I was about to get revealed that there was a lot more to this than one would think. Hard lessons as well as trial and error had made this simple procedure of flipping an art form, and I was about to be given the crash course on the basics.

"First thing, kid, drink plenty of soda. You're going to need it to push everything in your belly back up."

This introductory statement was followed by one lesson after another: Things like never eat chunky solid food as it hurts coming up, or avoid spaghetti as it can stick in your throat. As these facts started flying at me from all sides, I made a mental checklist. Pretty soon, one of the older guys took over and laid it all out.

"Eat 'til you feel like popping," he said pointing his fork at me, "as it will help when you reach for it. You drink your sodas and when you're loaded up hit the john and get yourself in a crouch; kinda like your riding position and just reach in and push on your tonsils a bit and the rest will happen."

Even though all the jocks seemed fine with the idea of flipping, some part of me wasn't. I knew it was wrong.

I didn't grow up in a household that tolerated wastefulness and really that's all flipping was; wastefulness.

Before the night was over, however, I decided to give it a try. I didn't feel comfortable having my first time trying it to be in a crowded restaurant so I decided to wait until I got home.

Leaving dinner, I stopped at a gas station and armed myself with the tools needed to perform the act. I didn't want to try anything solid because you never know how it will turn out, and God forbid I didn't drink enough soda and choked on something. Ice cream seemed the way to go. Two quarts of the stuff and a few sodas, and I was on my way.

Like most things in life, you never forget your first time. I downed all the supplies and headed to the bathroom. Assuming the position, I reached in and did as instructed.

For some reason, the ice cream, and most of my dinner, came up rather easily and the idiot kid in me realized that I could have the best of both worlds: I could eat what I wanted, and all I needed to do was flip.

The realization was like you see in cartoons when a good idea is had; a giant lightbulb lights up. It was very much like that, and the sad part is that the lightbulb would burn out, as would I over the coming years.

I think about that dinner so much. Looking back, it highlights how green I was to the life on the track and that of a jockey. Sure, guys were quick to tell me about flipping, and some even warned me about the long term effects, but, by then, I was in no position to listen to their advice, and really, it wasn't something I wanted to discuss with anyone, especially the people I had to compete with every day.

As a jock, you never want to show your weaknesses as it just sets you up for a fall when you do. When you compete in such a dangerous sport and in such tight quarters you learn the weaknesses of the other riders very fast, little things that might give you an edge when you're getting close to the wire. You know when guys are weak. You know when you can put them in positions they can't get out of because they're scared and will pull back. Because of this, there was no way I was going to talk about how flipping was starting to make me feel.

I know it sounds strange, but it really was just part of the game. I started flipping at home or in private. I managed to give the impression that I didn't actually do it at all. I got so crafty that the other riders believed I just stuck to a strick diet.

I'd become so good at hiding my "dieting skills" that I'd slipped into a very secretive world; a world that would lead to a very lonely existence.

My typical day would begin with a cup of strong coffee with three sugars to get the heart pumping, and then it was off to the track for morning work. The sweet coffee came in handy as it woke me up and made me sweat off a few pounds during the morning's work. Then it was off to the races to get through the day's calls and then, the Good Lord willing, home.

I never made flipping right before a race a habit as it made me feel dizzy. However, on occasion, I did do it and felt afterwards that I could've ridden better. I don't think it ever cost me a race. You know, when you're not one hundred percent you can easily put others in bad positions because you're not fully able to do your job. Its a bit like riding injured; it happens all the time but its really not right.

It was when I was at home and no prying eyes could see me that the hardest part of my day began. I tried to limit my flipping to nighttime as it was easier just to eat the one meal and pop a few sleeping pills and fall asleep and not deal with the headaches and dizziness that followed. It's sad, but over the years, I became like a mad scientist with the whole process. I learned which foods came up easier, or didn't sit too heavy on my stomach. I figured out which foods were hard or could choke you. The jockeys were right; spaghetti was the hardest to deal with.

Eventually, I learned that when I tasted the bitter taste of stomach acid that I had gotten all the contents out. This allowed me the opportunity of relaxing and going to sleep without the worry of having to spend hours in the sauna the next day. So, yes, flipping was my saving grace.

For the first few years flipping didn't seem to bother me, sure there were the headaches or bouts of dizziness when I overdid it, but all in all, it seemed to be the best way to eat and ride and not be driven crazy by a diet.

For me, the fact that the guys I looked up to seemed to be doing it made flipping seem more like the normal way of doing things. Yes, gorging yourself like a tick then sticking your finger down you throat and pulling the trigger was normal.

One thing leads to another; it's a saying that is probably as old as time, but in a world of bad habits it rang true. I'd been flipping for over a year when I started realizing that I wasn't able to get everything up anymore. I'm sure that my body was fighting me for every morsal as it wanted to keep enough so it could function, but I wanted to get everything out so I could play the game and ride.

Given all of this, laxatives soon followed. Like everything else I learned at this stage of my career, I had asked one of the older guys who was bigger in frame what he did. "You must do more than just flip to keep the weight off," I casually suggested to him one day. It was another question I could've lived without asking.

In the beginning, I popped a couple of laxative tablets just in case I didn't mange to empty my belly. The laxatives made sure that my system was cleared out before I had to report my weight.

Over the years, a couple of tablets became five or six just to get them to be effective. I imagine that it's like every other drug that you abuse; over time you develop a tolerance for it and need more and more of it for it to work. This was the case here. It's hard to write this as even now I feel stupid for falling into a lifestyle that led me down this path.

After three and a half years, things came to a head one day while I was preparing for a race. I finished using the "normal" toilet when I noticed a lot of blood in my stool. I'd seen bits of blood before and never thought much about it, but this was different. Yes, this was very different. There was so much blood that I nearly vomited looking at it.

Right then, I knew that I was at a crossroads. The years of bad diets and laxatives had caught up with me and I was staring at the result in the bowl below me.

I walked back to my locker. My valet, Danny, knew something was wrong. "What?" was all he said and then he added, "You look like you've seen a ghost."

I leaned into him and told him what had just happened, and the first thing he said was "you idiot, why didn't you tell me you were doing these things? I'm your valet, man. You need to talk to me. Remember the kid that died at Colonial years ago? Well, that's the same shit he was doing."

We sat there for a few minutes and thought about how best to deal with the situation. We agreed that seeing a doctor was the first move.

Climbing into my pick-up that night was hard because I knew that riding horses was slowly killing me.

As I drove home, I thought about everything that had happened to me in racing and wondered how I'd arrived at this point in my life.

*M*e in primary school; I was already
a gentleman and a scholar.

2

Starting Out

In Ireland, horses were always on TV as horse racing is a national pastime. I use to love watching them, especially the jump horses. Something about man and beast racing over fences just caught me and stayed with me. One horse in particular, Desert Orchid, was special to watch. He had heart and even as a kid I knew it. He would make these spectacular leaps and really attack his fences; he would either win, or go down trying. Even if he had four legs, for me, he became a serious role model.

Horses in Ireland are not hard to find; they are everywhere. They are nearly as numerous as the raindrops that keep our little island so green. The funny thing about my getting started with horses is that from the very beginning they scared me. My parents took a picture when I was seven sitting on a horse the day I made my First Communion. I was not very happy to be up there. Without being able to see that photograph, I never would've believed them.

As a kid, I enjoyed all the usual sports we played in Ireland, especially soccer. But, as my friends grew, and I didn't, riding horses started to seem like a sport I could fit into.

*M*y dad, Danny, had a cousin named Jimmy, who lived about thirty minutes from our home in Tipperary. He owned a pony trekking and fox hunting business. He had about thirty horses of all kinds, from the big strong hunters to the smallest pony.

Unlike things in the United States, in Ireland you can go up to places like this and rent out the horses or ponies for the day. You can get instruction or just go for a long ride, whatever you want you can do. It's hard seeing these places work in the States because of the liability issues, but at home these types of businesses are all over and luckily for me, Jimmy was family, so it made access to the horse world a little easier.

When I was thirteen years old, I asked my parents to let me go to Jimmy's for the summer to see if I could at least find my feet. They were a bit reluctant, but they finally agreed to let me go under one condition: If I didn't like it, there would be no more talk and pestering about riding, and I would knuckle down and concentrate on my school work.

My poor parents didn't know what they were letting themselves in for. They thought that over the summer Jimmy would work the crap out of me cleaning stalls and putting me on horses wild enough to buck me off the idea of making them my life. I know my mother, Breda, who I called mam, was worried. She was a timid woman who never got closer than ten feet to a horse without getting nervous. I'm sure she was not impressed with her only son wanting to go down this road.

As they drove away after dropping me off that day, I bet they thought that they would soon be getting a call saying I wanted to come home and I'd seen the light. Well, I did see the light just not the one they were expecting.

Jimmy was a great equestrian and had a very unique sense of humor, which I was often the brunt of. Most jokes involved how to get me to fall off horses. In those early days that didn't take much. There was never any intent on Jimmy's part to hurt me, but it was the Irish way of toughening me up.

Thinking back, I know it was Jimmy's way of setting me up for the life I dreamed with horses because he knew that for every jockey that came home a winner there were ten that came home smelling like dirt.

After that summer at Jimmy's, I knew for sure that I was no superstar on a horse, but I also knew that I was tough. A spark started to burn inside of me; a spark I never thought could be dimmed or put out.

At that age, all I knew was that the desire was there and for the first time in my life without daydreaming, I knew what I wanted to do, no questions asked.

Once summer was over, I grudgingly made my way into third year; the equivalent of the ninth grade in America.

At every opportunity, I voiced my hatred for school and told my parents that I should be off working in a racing yard, not wasting my time learning stuff that I would never use in my life.

They ignored me. They knew that at fourteen, I was in no position to tell them what was best for my future.

There was no way that my parents were going to let their only son drop out of school with no education to fall back on, armed with nothing but self-assurance and the dream of being a jockey.

I knew that Jimmy had told my parents how hard I'd worked over the summer. I just knew that they realized that there really was something driving me. I also knew that they were realists. If I was ever going to continue the journey down the road I was on, I knew I had to find a loophole.

To their credit, my parents did bring me up to Jimmy's over the weekends and after school they let me work on a farm near our house, where I did everything from mucking stalls to herding sheep just to get a shot of messing about on the few ponies they had at the place. While there was no one there to teach me anything about horses and riding; just being able to sit on a horse and using what I'd learned from Jimmy made me feel like I was starting to live my dream.

I was no longer concerned about being too small to play the sports I loved as a boy as I had found my calling. Now it was just a matter of getting my parents to come over to my way of thinking. I really believed that if I wanted something bad enough I would find a way of making it happen; it's a belief that I hold to this day.

I kept working on finding my loophole until finally, one day, I found what I'd been searching for. There was a jockey school just two-and-one-half hours from our house in Tipperary. The place was actually set up by the government to help produce top class jockeys to keep new blood coming into the game, and to top it all off, they helped aspiring jocks with their education.

I knew my parents would have a hard time finding something wrong with the idea of me going there.

I secured an application and brought it home to them. They listened and understood the fact that the school was designed to help a young person in all aspects of the horse racing game; be it riding in races or their education. They also knew that of the one hundred or so hopefuls that applied every year only twenty-five were selected and that out of that number, perhaps ten or fifteen would actually finish the ten-month course.

I explained that I fit the height and weight restrictions and impressed them with the fact that the school had produced numerous champion flat and steeplechase jockeys. By the grace of God, they agreed to let me try out, but once again the deal being that if I didn't make it, I would focus on school and put racing on hold.

My invite to the summer tryouts arrived in June 1995. The letter came in the mail, and I will never forget how excited I was to open it. To be honest it was the first official letter I'd ever received. The tryouts were to be held the week before my fifteenth birthday, and even though I had just one summer of experience with horses, here was my shot.

I knew going in I would do whatever it took to get into the school.

*W*orking, yes working, at mucking up stalls
during my days at Mickey Flynn's.

3

Educating Tom

The Racing Apprentice Center of Education, or R.A.C.E as it was called, was located in Kildare the very center of the horse racing world in Ireland. Kildare was the home of the Irish Derby, and approximately sixty-five percent of the country's leading trainers were based there. I remember the drive up with my father and mother. All I did was stare out the car's window beside me wondering about all the horses the place must have. I couldn't wait to get started.

When we arrived, my daydream of horses running free as far as the eye could see was replaced with reality. I was shocked to see that the campus looked like any other school I'd known and was trying to get away from.

For starters, there were no horses on the grounds, and the area was laid out like a boarding school; complete with adminstrative offices and a bunch of dorm room buildings.

Even so, I was not going to give up hope. We parked the car and eventually made our way to the orientation room where we joined thirty other kids and their parents. We were told that this was one of two or three trials to be held throughout the summer and that from these trials only a select number would be invited to attend the school's ten-month apprentice training program.

After orientation, I bid my parents goodbye.

For the first time in my life, I was on my own.

It was time to grow up and to do something with my life.

Like me, there were some kids who were really into the idea of making it as jockeys and were willing to do whatever it took. Then there were some who were there because of family connections and thought it was best to just go along. There were also a few who were there for no other reason than they had nothing better to do with their lives.

Our reasons for being there might have differed, but we all lived through the same routine everyday. We were up by dawn and worked like rented mules the rest of the day. Be it mucking out stalls at the nearby Irish National Stud or just running and exercising, we were kept busy all day. There were no snacks, and meals were served at a set time, plus there was little to no time spent on riding horses, which really upset me.

Discipline was big in the school. Smoking and staying up past curfew were not allowed. Sneaking off into town was a definite no-no. But, as you can imagine, with thirty teenagers none of these rules were followed to the letter. Some of the guys from Dublin's inner city were a little more streetwise than most of us from the country, and they seemed to have no problem sneaking out at night to go to the store for chocolate and other things that were not allowed on school grounds.

For a price, you could get one of the kids to go to the store to buy anything you needed. The going price was the equivalent of a dollar, a charge that was added to the cost of the merchandise you ordered, so a guy going out for ten or more kids a few times a week had a nice little racket going on. The only problem was if you were caught, it was over. No excuses, just pack your things and climb aboard a bus home.

For two weeks, this trial went on, and there were plenty who sank because they couldn't take the work or the exercise or because they got busted doing runs to the store. Whatever the reason, by the end of the two weeks our numbers had dwindled, but me, I had made it.

Now it was a case of waiting to see if I had been accepted into the school's ten-month program.

Once again, the deal with my parents stood; if I didn't get in I would go back and focus on school, and there would be no more talk about racing.

Like all things that are meant to be, I was selected for the program: My life with horses was about to begin in earnest.

On the first day of the course, we were weighed and measured; a rite that turned out to be a weekly ritual. As was the case before, some of the kids that got into the program were not from horse backgrounds. The one summer at Jimmy's place had given me a slight edge the first few weeks, but it all evened out over time. As we started to work and tried to survive, our differences became less and less, as we were thrown into a world that we were not sure how to handle.

The course was broken into two parts. The first part consisted of us training at an army base where they kept retired showjumpers. These beasts would be our training tools for the next three months. The army corporals who were there to train us didn't care who we were or where we came from. No, they had a spartan idea that the strong survive and the weak go home to their mommies. Believe me this was tough and over the period we were there, we had quite a few wash out and quit.

The corporals had seen groups come and go and really had their strategy for training down to an art. There was no, "lets start slow and try to find your way." It was all, "Get on! Don't fall off and get on with it!" We were put on these ex-showjumpers. At the time they seemed to all of us like huge animals that seemed so strong, but they knew their jobs, and we just had to stay on them.

We were drilled inside this big, dusty indoor arena. With fifteen horses jogging around at the same time, the dust in the place got thick. We rode in two sets; fifteen would watch and fifteen would ride. I always thought it was better to be picked in the first group as then you had a little excuse for not understanding what they were asking you to do.

The corporals seemed to throw more helmets and curses at the second group, because in their way of thinking if a kid was in the second group, they should have learned from watching the mistakes made by the first group. If their logic was correct, then all we needed to do was go watch tons of videos of races, and we would all become great jockeys.

The big horses we rode were kind to us. These animals, who had been trained and ridden by the army's best riders for most of their careers and had competed all over the world, were now in their glorious retirement, being flopped around on by these pint-sized beginners. I don't say "ridden by" because at this stage all we could do was flop around.

These big monsters were like lambs with us. Sure, we fell off them, but it was never because they were being malicious. No, these gentle giants were kind, and for that reason, I never forgot them.

The army part was very tough and as one might expect we learned some colorful adjectives. One corporal had been injured in the Congo during the sixties and talked really funny. When he got mad, his words got scrambled, and he would spit while shouting his favorite word, "motherfucker!" Looking back it was funny, but at the time getting him mad enough to scream at you was pretty intimidating.

It was through this part of the program that we started losing people. Some just couldn't take the shouting and the throwing of helmets at them when a corporal thought they were not up to scratch. Still others left after they were hurt.

In those early days, we really didn't know how to take a fall. When we came off a horse most of us were apt to put out our hands to save ourselves. Big mistake, as it was the fastest way to break a wrist. Later we learned that you should tuck and roll, but in the beginning, we didn't know that. It took its toll. Out of the thirty that had started, there were twenty-three of us left standing by the end of this phase of our training.

After this, it was on to Part Two where we were sent out to work for different trainers during the mornings. I was one of three sent to the barn of the famous trainer Dermot Weld, one of Ireland's most successful race horse trainers. In August 2000, Weld set the record for the most winners trained in Ireland with two thousand five hundred and seventy-eight. The idea here was to immerse us into the world of a racing stable.

I lasted three days at Weld's. A filly ran off with me, and the assistant, an old miserable man called Jackson, told me I would never make it in this game, and I should go back to regular school. He called the Center and said he didn't want to keep me. My world would've been so much different if he had had his way.

Usually when a person was kicked off a job, they were sent home. Luckily, one of the instructors at the Center was friends with a trainer by the name of Mickey Flynn. The instructor gave him a call and Mickey was willing to take me on.

Not long before, Mickey had gotten a filly from Weld that he was told was untrainable, and she was now flying, so I imagine he thought he could do the same for me.

My first morning at Flynn's was so much different than Weld's. People were working faster as there was less staff and still the same amount of work to be done. The head lad told me where the forks and brushes were and told me to just start mucking stables. By day's end, I'd cleaned all thirty of them on my own.

Mickey checked on my work and said very little at all. This went on every day for a week and even though it was not exactly what I wanted to be doing, in my mind, it was so much better than washing out and having to go back to normal school.

On my second Monday at Flynn's, I was making my way to grab my fork and brushes when Mickey stopped me and said, "Grab that spare saddle inside and someone will help you get the horse in box twenty-three tacked up."

I was delighted. Stall twenty-three belonged to a smallish little bay called Mile a Minute, a horse who was known as Miley. He was a hurdle horse that at this particular time was starting over chase fences, but compared to most other race horses he was as quiet as a pony and was a favorite of everyone because of his gentle nature.

All Mickey told me was to sit still and Miley would do the rest. The horse did, and unlike at Weld's, I survived my first day riding out for a real trainer.

Over the weeks that followed Miley was my only mount. I thought of him as *my* first real race horse, and I dreamed of riding him in big races. Every morning when we galloped, the markers along the way became imaginary finish lines, and we always won. That was the great thing about dreams, I never finished second.

As time went by, I started getting on more horses, but Miley would always be my favorite. It was thanks to him that I really knew that I had made the right career choice. Maybe if Miley was mean, I wouldn't have lasted, but something about him seemed almost human to me, and he was my first real friend in racing.

After riding Miley for a few weeks, Mickey allowed me to ride some of the other horses and school older ones over hurdles. He bought a three-quarter Thoroughbred pony to teach me to jump over the bigger fences because he didn't want to have me mess up on a paying customer's horse. This pony was awesome. He didn't even have a name we all just called him "the pony." He was fast as well and could layup with most horses in the yard.

All in all, Mickey taught me a lot, and he set me up for going out into the world on my own. He was a hard taskmaster but a fair one. He came up through the ranks by working hard, and it had worked out well for him. He had been a successful jockey and now he had thirty-five horses in training. He would be the first to tell you if you did a good job, but also the first to put a boot in your rear if you didn't.

From Mickey we learned respect, respect for the horses, because, as he so often reminded us, without them we didn't have a job. We also learned respect for ourselves. He would always say that we needed to look the part if we were to be the part.

Along the way, Mickey also made sure to point out the little things from tucking in your shirt, to having the correct manners when owners came to visit their horses. It was all important as you couldn't have one without the other. We needed horses, but more importantly, we needed owners to pay for them. All of these things added up to being a successful jockey. Above all, Mickey taught us how to carry ourselves in public.

Yes, the grounding I learned from Mickey helped a lot over the years, especially when I went to America where how you conducted yourself opened doors for you.

Finally, after six months, I graduated from R.A.C.E. I believe there were eighteen of us who completed the course. For the graduation ceremony, we were all dressed up in our school uniforms and were presented with our diplomas.

My parents came up for the day. They were proud of the fact that I'd made it through the program and was now ready to pursue a career as a jockey. They never said it, but at the time, I also felt that they were proud of the fact that I was a hardworking kid who understood the difference between a pipe dream and reality.

Mickey also took the time to be at the graduation ceremony. Maybe he felt a bit of special pride in the fact that I was graduating. After all, if it hadn't been for his intervention six months before my dream of being a jockey would've been over. Mickey believed in me and for that I would never let him down.

Following graduation, it was left up to us to find our way. There was no placement officer, or counselor waiting to give us advice on where to find a job. It was sink or swim.

I was fortunate in that Mickey offered me a full-time job. With nobody else beating down my door, I gladly accepted.

I was sixteen and had a job I loved and was learning more and more every day. In time, Miley won his first race over chase fences. I remember being on top of the world. I wasn't his jockey, but I got to go to the track where I led him around the parade ring.

A few days after the race, I received another lesson in racing when Miley's jockey for the race, Anthony Powell, came by the stable to see how the horse was doing. It was just a class thing to do. I was awestruck. Here was this guy that rides big races every day driving into our yard in his big shiny car just to see how a horse he won a small race on was doing.

What struck me even more was the fact that before he left, he came over to me and slipped fifty pounds into my hand. "Thanks for looking after him kid." That's all he said, "Thanks for looking after him kid," and he was off to some other barn to either ride or check on other horses.

Later, I asked Mickey why Mr. Powell had done that and all Mickey said was "Poweller, he's old school."

Well, I liked his school, and it dawned on me then that you should always take care of the people behind the scenes who do the hard work every day and don't get their names in the paper.

At the time, Keiran Kelly was the stable's apprentice, and Mickey looked at him almost like a son. Keiran was a great guy to work with, quick to play a joke when the time was right, but the first to know the time and place for everything. He was two years out of the apprentice school and he was far ahead of everyone I knew. Whether it was his style on a horse, or how easy he made everything look, there was just something about him that was cool.

Being a kid, Keiran was the guy I looked up to and tried to model myself after. Keiran's big ride at the time was a filly called Angel From Heaven and she would go on to be his first winner as a jockey. The funny thing about this filly was that she was the filly Mickey had gotten from Weld because she was "untrainable."

Looking back, I realize Weld got a few predicitons wrong.

After Keiran rode Angel From Heaven to his first win, we all celebrated. Mickey was so happy as he had trained the rider and the filly, a filly who was thought of as untrainable, and yet, the both of them had reached the winner's circle.

In Ireland, an apprentice "signs on" for three years with his trainer which means that the trainer has first call on the rider for three years and will help him get his career going in return.

Soon after his first win, Keiran signed on with Mickey. I was happy for him, but I knew at that moment that I would have to move on, as Mickey didn't have enough horses in training to support two apprentices.

Even so, I didn't leave right away as I had so much more to learn and I knew this was the best place for me to earn my education. It was great. One guy, we called "Doc" would come in to ride out on weekends when he was home from college and afterwards we would all go out on Saturday nights. "Doc" and Keiran bought me my first drink of alcohol. It was called a "mule." It was some kind of vodka mixed drink. It was terrible, but it made me feel like I belonged.

"Doc" and Keiran also set up my first sexual experience, and no, not in the paying for it sense. They just knew a girl that was, well, for want of a better word, liberal.

These were good times, but as with all things, life soon propelled us down the road. Eventually, Mickey left training horses, preferring to break them and do pretraining. Kerian became a top Irish jump jockey, and it looked like the world was his for the taking. Sadly, he died on August 12, 2003, a few days after he was injured in a fall at Kilbeggan race track. He was only twenty-five years old.

Altogether, the life I had lived up to this point made me feel as if I'd made the right choice in my future career. I was now sixteen years old and loving life. The day I would get to ride in real races seemed like it would come before too long if I stuck with it.

I would.

I wanted nothing more.

*O*nly seventeen, but already looking
like a seasoned professional.

4

Off to *America*

During the winter of 1997, pre-paid cell phones were all the rage in Ireland. I had bought one, and one night I dialed a number in America just to see if my phone could actually reach the States. I called a number listed on an advertisement in one of the racing papers. The ad read that they were looking for a young person to work and ride the races in America. I talked to someone who said he was a trainer. He told me the job was taken but that he would keep my number anyway.

"No worries," I said. I was never really expecting anything to come out of the call, I was just happy to discover that my cheap cell phone could reach America.

It's funny what amused me back then.

I moved on from Mickey's that winter as I felt I was closer to the point where race riding was the next step. I tried another barn but I wasn't happy there, and then one night, almost like magic, my cell phone rang. It was a Friday night to be exact. "Is this Tom?" the voice on the other end asked.

"Yes it is," I answered.

"Tom this is Jimmy Day here. You called me a few months back asking about a job and well, that guy didn't work out. Are you still interested?"

"Sure," was all I could say, but I remember that I said it in a way that sounded like I'd been expecting his call and wondered what had taken him so long.

In reality, I was caught completely off-guard, I mean here was a guy telling me I could ride right away; the one thing I wanted the most.

I agreed to go but there were a couple of problems. This was Friday night, and he needed me there on Monday; as in two days time! Then, there was the small matter of convincing my parents to let me go.

Funny how things never turn out how you expect. I mean, here I was expecting an all out "no" even before I finished asking my parents, and as it turned out they were saying "yes" and offering their blessing before I'd finished asking for permission; amazing how life works that way.

Looking back on it, I figure they probably didn't have much time to think it over as it was sprung on all of us on such short notice. Maybe if we had had more time to think it over I never would've gotten on the plane, but it's one of those things that just happened so fast that it just seemed to flow on. What I remember the most about the conversation though was when my dad told me that he knew how hard I'd been working and how he didn't want to stand in the way of my dreams.

So that was it. I was off to America. Race riding was just an airplane ride away.

Dad drove me to the airport. We didn't talk about anything much out of the ordinary on the way up, mostly about local sporting teams. My mother didn't come with us as we all knew it would be too hard for her to leave me at the airport without knowing what lay in store for me. At that point in her life, I think my mother had just been on a plane once when my parents went to England for their honeymoon. I think the flight was thirty minutes so for her son to be taking a six-hour flight to a place where he knew no one was a bit too much.

As for my sisters, they were both in school at the time. The youngest, Ruth, was probably glad to be rid of me, while the eldest, Valerie, was just starting her first year in college so I'm pretty sure I wasn't at the top of her priority list. Either way, I imagine they thought I was going for a few weeks and would get lonely and return home. I probably would've been thinking the same thing if I were them, but this was my shot to ride, and I was taking it.

When my dad and I finally reached the airport, things got a little more emotional as my takeoff was closing in. This was in the days before 911 so my dad was able to go with me to the gate. We were never really a very lovey-dovey family. I mean, we all knew we loved and cared deeply for each other, but we were not the types to go around saying it to each other every day.

As leaving drew closer, I could tell it was hard on my dad. He played it off as a man in this situation would. When the time came to board my plane, he wished me luck, and we hugged and then he said, "Take care." That was it.

He had a little tear in his eye, and I knew when he got back to the car and was on his own that it would hit him harder, but for now he held it together. I wasn't too sad as on my end. I was excited in knowing that my dream of race riding was just a plane ride away.

I'd never been on a plane before and really didn't know what to expect. In Ireland, I was so sheltered from so much of life's diversity. I remember being five or six years old and seeing my first black person in the flesh. I mean we have different ethnicities in some of the big cities in Ireland, but we hardly visited them when I was a child. No, this poor guy was in doing a little shopping when this pint-sized freckly faced kid came running up to him screaming, "Its Benson! Look Daddy, it's Benson!!"

Benson was a character in a television show that we used to watch. He was cool, and in my mind here he was right in front of me in our local store. To say my dad was embarrassed is an understatement, and I can't remember how the other man felt. I hope he at least remembers the story with a laugh and took it for what it was, an innocent kid who hadn't seen enough of the world to know better.

Leaving home was weird for me in many ways. It didn't quite hit me until I got on the plane, and I realized that it was happening right now; right here, right in front of me.

After a while, I don't know why, but I thought of the kids who were standout sports players in what would be high school for us in Ireland. I thought of how when high school was over they lived on their reputation for years, or until someone else younger and better came along to steal their thunder and that was it, peaked by eighteen.

I didn't want that for me. I didn't want to be the guy in a pub reliving the glory days every weekend and then waking up and remembering it was twenty years ago.

It goes without saying that I would miss Ireland as it was all I knew; but, I also knew that if I stayed put I would always wonder what might've been.

I thought about things like this on the plane, and as I looked out over the Atlantic, I smiled because I knew, even then, that this was the part of living that I loved the most; the part of never really knowing what tomorrow would bring.

I didn't sleep on the plane as I was far too excited for that. When we landed at Dulles International Airport, some twenty-six miles from downtown Washington, D.C., it was another culture shock as I'd never seen so many different people in one place. I was awestruck. It just seemed so big and everyone seemed in a hurry.

Eventually, Jimmy Day and his wife picked me up. Jimmy was from Ireland as well. He had been a jockey in Ireland who had come to America when he was in his twenties to try and ride the American circuit. I'm not sure how well he did as a rider, but he seemed at home as a trainer.

As I was to discover, Jimmy kept his barn very much like the Irish trainers do at home. I guess that's why he liked getting help from Ireland as he knew we would fit in easier to the way he did things.

Jimmy and his wife seemed nice enough. We talked a little on our way back to his farm. Jimmy wanted to know more about my riding experience. From the sound of it, he was thinking of putting me on some horses at a point to point race the coming Saturday.

Point to point races gave horses and jockeys an opportunity to gain experience. These races didn't count towards a jockey's official count of victories or on a horse's form.

He dropped me off at his farm with the girl who lived there. We were to be roommates. Her name was Michelle. She was a fair bit older than me, and her long red hair and freckles reminded me of the girls and women I knew in Ireland. She was nice to me and from talking to her I understood that she was used to people coming and going from the barn so some random kid showing up to be her new roommate was nothing new. She asked me if I was hungry which I was as I didn't eat much on the plane. She drove me to a McDonalds. At the time I thought it was awesome as we only had McDonalds restaurants in major cities at home, and I'd only eaten in a few so this was a real treat.

After a month, McDonalds lost its charm; another case of too much of a good thing.

The day after I arrived, I had my first chance at riding an American Thoroughbred. The first thing I noticed was that American horses pulled harder than the ones at home. In Ireland, we have horses bred for the flat and also for steeplechase. They are all Thoroughbreds but the faster ones will be bred from speedier families and the bigger slower types will go on to jumping. However, over here, it was a case of after their flat career the horses were sent jumping so they had started out going over shorter distances and were now trying a new game; one that went for a further distance and included jumping over a variety of fences and riding over different terrain.

The following Saturday, I not only rode in my first race, I rode in three. Jimmy named me on two flat horses in novice rider races and on one horse over hurdles. They were not sanctioned races just point to point, the races that were meant to educate young horses and young riders. I suppose they are akin to bush racing in Louisiana.

The days leading up to that weekend were a blur. Jimmy kept telling me things that he thought would help and really his suggestions went in one ear and out the other. I guess when you spend so long wanting just one single thing when you get close to realizing it you just seem to zone out any advice given to you. I knew that these were not real races and that they wouldn't count, but they were races nonetheless, and they were my first. I would be lying if I said I wasn't nervous.

As he gave me a leg up for my first race, Jimmy gave me my final instructions. "Just sit in," he offered, "and make a move the last quarter of a mile. Whatever you do don't be up close to the pace."

So now, here I was thinking, okay, I've got my orders, and I will just pop-off and follow them, but it didn't turn out to be that easy. There were seven horses in the race, and nobody seemed to want to make the running or be in front so here we had pretty much every novice rider who had been given the same instructions all trying to do what they were told but now were all fighting their horses to do so. It was a mess. My horse pulled so hard that my arms and legs were numb by the time we finished. No amount of morning exercise will get you fit to ride races you just need to go out and keep doing it.

After all was said and done, I managed to finish in second. As I rode back to Jimmy, I could tell he looked a bit confused. He asked why I didn't go to the front when there was no pace to follow. I said I thought he wanted me to hold the horse up, and he laughed. "I can only tell you what might happen," he said shaking his head, "and how to try and do it if it works out according to plan, but you need to be able to think for yourself when it's not going your way."

He was right, and I knew it. Sometimes you just need to switch on the brain. He handled the situation well as he knew it was my first attempt, and I would get better. It was a valuable lesson to learn; maybe if I'd won by twenty lengths I might have missed it, but it's the mistakes and getting things wrong that makes us better.

I finished third in my second race. I enjoyed it but the third race was over fences and that is what I'd dreamed about doing ever since I'd wanted to become a jockey. I know it must seem odd to want the first two races of your career out of the way just so you can get to that third one, but really that was how it went. I guess I was a little different even back then.

My last mount of the day was named Be a Contender. Like me, he was having his first run over hurdles. Everything in the race was going great early on. The flag dropped, and we settled into a nice rhythm in the middle of the pack. We covered the first circuit with no problem, and I remember racing down to my first fence knowing this is the moment I'd been dreaming about since I was a boy.

When Be a Contender launched over the fence, and I managed to stay with him it seemed like I was at home. It was such a rush. I'd never jumped a fence on a horse going that fast before; well maybe I did, but when so much is going on around you all at once everything just seemed so much faster. You're trying to keep position and make sure your horse sees each fence, and all these things happening that you're not used to. It gets easier over time, and it becomes second nature, but that first time you're just lost as its nothing like anything you have experienced.

It is funny though, because as all this was happening, I was wondering what mam and dad were doing at that same moment. They had no idea that at that second I'd jumped my first fence, and the road was being paved for what would be this story. It's strange I know, but it's what I thought after we landed safely. Like I said, I am a little different.

Be a Contender and I had a great trip going and as we approached the second to the last jump, we ran down to it and he left the ground to jump right on queue. The next thing I knew, I was sitting on the ground watching him gallop off with the other runners. For the first time, I realized how quickly things happen in races; one second you can be flying and the next you can be sitting on the ground. It was a hard lesson as it felt like my first winner was so close. I knew that it wouldn't have been a real winner in terms of professional racing, but when you're just starting out your career every race feels like the Irish Derby.

For me, however, it was the first ride that woke me up to the idea that racing was tough and to make it, you had to be tougher; even tougher than I'd been taught.

I stayed with Jimmy for over a year and eventually rode my first winner for him in another point to point race outside Washington D.C. It was the feature. I remember getting to see my name in *The Washington Post* in a small article, which seemed like a huge deal at the time: "Deal Again and Foley Win Preakness Hurdle" was the caption. I couldn't wait to send the article home to my parents.

Deal Again was super cool. He was an old horse and knew more about the game than I did by far. He was from New Zealand, and I'm not sure who Jimmy got him from but he thought after my fall in the first race that I needed to ride something safe; something that knew how to adjust if I made a green mistake. He was right. This old guy was a pro and just took off at the perfect spot every time.

When you're young and you win any race it feels like you just won the Derby. It didn't matter if it was a point to point, to me I'd won my first race, and that is special forever. Sure it wasn't a professional meet, but in my mind right then I'd made it.

The day I left Weld's to go work for Mickey seemed so far away. It all seemed worth it at that moment and really isn't that why I was riding in the first place, to get that feeling? At least for me right then that way of thinking made sense and that feeling would become my life; a life spent chasing it; then when I caught it, I tried to do it all over again.

Winning, it's great until it's gone. Then what do you chase? I wish the answer to that question was simple, but, as I learned over time, it wasn't.

I did think it was good of Jimmy to put me on Deal Again because he was not short on choices of jockeys but he gave me another shot, and I will always be grateful to him for that.

Jimmy was probably a decent fellow, but for some reason we never clicked. Maybe I was younger than he expected and in his rush to get help over, he forgot that I was just seventeen and very green to the world. I did learn things from him and he did help me get that initial experience, but it never felt quite right. When you're that far from home and mostly on your own you need someone who can talk to you and try to understand how it might feel from the other side, but we never had that. He had his own kids, and I am sure that in his mind he didn't need another one.

My time with Jimmy ended quite abruptly. In October 1998, he had me signed on a horse named Last Hurrah, and this time it was in a professional meet at Morven Park in Virginia.

Last Hurrah was a funny sort of horse. We called him Buckey, not because he was a kids' pony, but because he was aggressive and had a temper that he was never afraid to let you see. He had this big dish head almost like an Arabian, but way bigger. He was not the easiest ride on the place but I liked him. Jimmy knew that, and somehow he talked the owners into giving me a shot. Well, they did, and the opportunity turned out to be life altering.

I was having a great trip, and the race was unfolding the way Jimmy and I had discussed. Last Hurrah and I were held up early and were making a move down the backstretch the final time around when we came to the next to the last hurdle. I remember sitting on a ton of horse but that was the last I remembered.

Last Hurrah's take off was too early, and he landed on the fence. He catapulted me to the ground on the other side and landed on me covering the lower half of my body. My chest and head were exposed and the horses jumping behind us landed on me. One of them crushed my sternum and broke my ribs and another put his hoof right through my chin and opened it up the whole length of my jaw.

To say I was in a bad state would be an understatement. My heart had stopped and luckily the vet who was tending to Last Hurrah knew CPR. He revived me to a point where my heart was beating again. (I've actually never met the man. His name was Doug Berry so after all of these years thanks Doug.)

I was rushed to a nearby hospital where I was in a coma for close to a week. Unfortunately, Last Hurrah didn't fare as well. He was killed by the fall.

I don't think Jimmy talked to my parents during any of this. Only when I was conscious did a friend of mine make contact with them to say I was doing fine. They were worried, but they could tell by my voice that I was going to be okay. My dad wanted to come over, but I talked him out of it. I would be fine; bones heal and stitches come out. If this was the life I'd chosen to go after then I would have to get used to it; we would all have to get use to it.

I still have the scar on my chin, and every now and then, I rub it just to remind myself how close I came to dying. Sometimes, I think of Kieran. I wonder why he died and I'd made it when my fall was far worse. It's just the way you land and that split second when horses' hooves are flying over you, or on you. It just depends on the second.

When I got out from the hospital and went back to work for Jimmy, things were different. Maybe he had gotten the heat for letting me ride the race and talking the owners into putting me on Last Hurrah. Maybe he was mad at me because the horse was killed. I'm not sure of the reason but he was mad. Little things I did began to bother him, like missing a cobweb when I was sweeping up the barn.

It was all starting to get to me too. After a month, I had enough. One evening, I just packed my bags and left. I didn't say a word to Jimmy; I needed out and maybe I just beat him to the punch. I do regret the way I left and would do it differently today, but when you're a kid you never know all the answers and well, you fuck up, very simple. I did, and well, I guess I can never change it.

It's easy to look back and see the whole story but when you're living it and trying to move up the ladder you just see your side. That's life, and you live with your decisions good and bad.

I wasn't worried about finding another chance to ride. After all, this was America, the land of opportunity, and I wasn't going to stop looking until I found my next one.

*M*e, Eddie Graham, the Thoroughbred,
Corruption, and all the joy of a jockey starting out.

5

The Wonder Years

Moving on from Jimmy Days, I decided to stay in Virginia. By now, I was eighteen years old, and the circuit in Virginia was all I really knew. I was still trying to make an impression; still trying to find that bit of luck that could springboard my career up the ladder to bigger things.

I refer to this time as the Wonder Years; a time when I saw things happening, but was never one hundred percent sure of what they meant or how to handle them.

For instance, in the midst of trying to find a place to live and horses to ride, I learned that my dad had suffered a heart attack and was in the hospital back in Ireland. I didn't have enough money to go home so I had to wait it out. My sisters kept me informed on his condition.

With my father in the hospital, I was a mess. I couldn't concentrate on anything, much less keep up. This was a problem, as I needed my mind focused on just two things; finding horses to ride and winning.

I tried to keep my head straight, but I kept thinking about dad and me not being there for him. Even though my sisters told me that he was going to be okay, I needed to see it for myself so I could deal with it and keep going.

I was riding in a point to point race a few days after finding out about my dad, and my mind was not there. I was leading and took the wrong course and kept going.

As I crossed the finish line, I thought I'd won, when in reality I was disqualified. I'd gotten lost and cut around the wrong flag. As it was the first time I'd done something like that, the stewards at the meet said nothing more than for me to know the course before I rode a race and to never let it happen again.

I was so embarrassed and between that and not really knowing how my dad was doing I was a mess. It's times like these that you question yourself as to where you're going in life. Here I was four-thousand miles from home and not really going anywhere in my career.

To make matters worse, I was losing races that don't count by getting lost and all the while my dad was sick at home.

It got to me.

After a few weeks, my dad was finally released from the hospital. We chatted over the phone and as is his style, he laughed off his heart attack, but I could tell that it hurt him. I could hear it in his voice. Just like that day when he left me at the airport, I could tell that he was just being strong for the both of us.

In the weeks following my conversation with my dad, I was riding a really tough little horse at the Warrenton races which was another point to point in Virginia. This little horse had no mouth and just wanted to bolt. I will never forget his name, Key to the Dungeon. I remember thinking, how can something this small be this out of control? Even so, I was sure I could at least get him to steer in the right direction and get him around the hurdle course.

The flag dropped and we set off a million miles an hour. He was flying. Having learned from experience that you need something left in the tank by the end of a race, I tried to hold him up a little during the early part of the course, but there was no slowing him down. I could steer okay, but it was his speed that I could do nothing about.

We jumped five fences then the course could go left or right, and I chose left, but as I turned up I knew I was wrong. We were meant to turn left the final time.

Now I'd finished up a circuit early and everyone could see my horse was still full of run and they could find no reason why I was there looking at them.

The stewards called me up to talk, and I told them my horse was so strong and he'd bolted with me going around the turn, therefore going the wrong direction.

As I was so far in front, it could've been a plausible excuse, but they knew the truth as did I. As it's not professional racing, there was nothing they could do to me. They couldn't suspend me or stop me from riding, so I felt I'd gotten away with what had happened.

At the time there was a steeplechase jockey named Gregg Ryan. He was the coolest jockey of us all, at least in relation to the point to point world I'd been riding in Virginia. He always had a neat car and the women loved him.

When I'd met him at seventeen, Gregg was the guy I looked up to for all the reasons most seventeen-year-olds would. Let's be honest, at that age you want to ride races and chase girls. It's the perfect life.

Gregg was in his mid-thirties at this stage of his career and had been a successful jockey for many years and ridden in all the big steeplechase races across America. Now, he was slowing down by riding where he felt at home and where he could ride among the people who had gotten him started. The concept was so alien to me back then. I mean if I would've had the opportunity to ride good horses in the best races that's what I would've been doing.

I simply couldn't understand why Gregg was wasting time riding in races that meant nothing.

After all, they didn't count.

I didn't quite get why he was there, but I was glad he was.

Anyway, having lied to the stewards, I returned to the jocks' tent where I was met by Gregg. He asked me what had happened and what I told the stewards. I told him I'd gone off course because I didn't know the right direction, but I also told him what I'd told the stewards. It was at this moment that I got my first glimpse of the real Gregg Ryan.

Up to this point, I thought of Gregg as nothing but a jock who loved to ride races and party. A couple of times he had invited me to his house for parties after the races, and it really was the place to be. Everybody was there: trainers, jockeys and 99% of the pretty women in northern Virginia. Gregg was a successful businessman and racing was his hobby so I felt like he could afford to just play the game any way he pleased.

"You learn something new everyday with horses." That saying is as old as the horse industry itself, and today I was about to learn something from Gregg Ryan that I would never forget.

After I finished telling Gregg what happened with the stewards, his face just seemed to get hard as he told me that in life people will forgive you for making mistakes and poor decisions if at least you can look them in the eye and say you're wrong. He then added that they will put up with only so much, but they will never put up with a liar. Sure they might have a drink with you or hang out with you, but they will never trust you, and then he asked me the question that has stuck with me since that day, "Is that the man you want to be?"

I thought about what he said and as he walked away, I turned around, walked back up to the stewards' tower and told them the truth as to what had really happened. They already knew but I think they were happy to know I could come clean and be man enough to admit I was wrong.

I didn't know that Gregg was watching me as I did this. He later told me that this was the moment he knew I was someone worth more of his time than just hanging out at the races and meeting up at the occasional party. Later on, he also told me that people can admit that they are wrong in private but doing it in public takes courage and that it takes a type of courage that will shape a life not the courage that it takes to guide a horse around a track.

After this, Gregg took a serious interest in me. He became a cross between a big brother and a father to me.

I could go on and on about the things Gregg taught me, but the lesson that has always stayed with me was to keep moving forward. There were so many guys who came over from Ireland or England who were much older and were just looking for a place to settle down. Sure, they had weekday jobs and they rode the points to points on the weekends as it made for a decent living, but at eighteen or nineteen, he taught me that I should want more than that. I didn't have the problem of wanting to settle down, but I needed help in remembering to keep pushing myself up the ladder of success.

I'd been in the United States for two years now and it was time to move up. I'd ridden enough to know how to win and look good doing it. Now, I needed an established trainer to give me a shot. Between Gregg and trainer Donny Yovanivich, who had given me a lot of chances to ride in the points to points, they made contact with Bruce Miller, a trainer who at the time was the leading trainer of steeplechase horses in America. They told Bruce they knew a kid who would work and was worth a shot if he needed an apprentice.

Bruce came down to Virginia and took me to lunch. He asked a lot of questions about me and what I wanted to do with my career.

I told him that I wanted to make my living riding horses and that before my career was over, I wanted to ride in Grade One races and win championships. I made sure to point out that these were dreams, but that I wasn't a dreamer. I was a realist who understood that it took hard work and determination to achieve goals.

Bruce sat listening, and when lunch was over he said, "Okay, grab your gear. You may as well come back to Pennsylvania with me now if you're going to do all those things."

It was as simple as that.

After two years of banging my head against a wall, I was finally going to a place where they had horses that, if I got a chance to ride, could make me a success.

Going to Miller's was a huge turning point for me in so many ways. Bruce talked to his horses and not in the way Monty Roberts claims to get into their heads and know their thoughts. No, Bruce literally talked to them. He made silly voices with different horses and seemed to know all their personalities. He just loved them.

I soon learned there was a huge difference between being a jockey and being a horseman. Bruce was a real horseman, who took care of his horses physically and mentally. For Bruce, it wasn't just about winning.

When I went there I was just glad to be going somewhere that I could get on some better horses than the ones I'd been riding in Virginia the past three years. I mean, I'd been in the Old Dominion State for this long and had yet to win a race under rules or as a professional. The point to point races were just practice and didn't count, so nothing I'd won really meant anything.

Bruce's assistant, Eddie Graham, and I didn't get off to a great start as he thought, and rightfully so, that all I cared about was winning races.

For a few weeks, Eddie was very cool with me and hardly said much until one day he just asked me "do you get it?"

"Get what?" I asked.

"It's not about you, man," he said squaring up to me, "or winning. It's about taking care of these guys and keeping them right. You keep a horse fit and happy and he wins races. Very simple, but if you can't see past yourself, to them, you will never win, there's a lot more going into this than just who finishes first."

I think he knew from the look on my face that I understood what he was telling me. I'd let my frustration and overeagerness to win stop me from seeing the big picture. Sometimes in life to go faster you need to slow down. I'm not sure if anyone has ever said that but they probably should have.

After my talk with Eddie and watching Bruce work for a few weeks, I started finding myself looking at horses differently. I started talking to them just like Bruce.

I soon realized that my attitude toward them had changed without my even knowing it. I thought about Miley and the other fine horses I'd ridden over the years. I remembered the joy of riding for the sheer love of doing it, but I also came to realize that riding was now my profession. If I was going to survive, it was going to be on the back of a horse, and the better the horse, the better my chances of making a paycheck.

But, what I could never let myself forget was that horses weren't tools. They were alive, and, like us, each of them were different.

Aside from adjusting my attitude toward horses, Bruce and Eddie started to help me with my patience.

They would tell me the horses knew when you're too anxious and that they felt it.

"You need to relax to win," they would say. "It's all about keeping calm under pressure."

To say they were part trainers and part Mr. Miyagi would be an accurate description.

My newfound approach to racing manifested iteself in a horse named Apache Twist, a horse that I will never forget. He was a quirky little horse that Bruce had bought in Ireland a few years before I'd arrived at this place and to be fair he had done well but had never won a race since coming to America. To say he had more seconds than a clock would be a better description, but he had never managed to get his nose in front. It didn't matter if it was a claimer or a stakes race he just didn't want to put his head in front.

Bruce liked to jog his horses a lot before they galloped and would take them, with their riders still up, for long walks home to cool them down. It was on one of these walks that he told me he was putting me on Apache Twist in a race coming up in a week or so. He said that he didn't think the horse was anything special, but that he was experienced and a good jumper and he would be a good ride for me.

"I will win on him, boss," I said with a smile, "just watch."

Bruce laughed and said, "If you win on him, I'll give you my ten percent of the purse as well as your own."

"Fair enough," I said and the bet was on.

It's funny to think a trainer would place a wager on his horse not winning even though he really wanted him to.

Apache Twist had just finished second too many times that Bruce just seemed to think he would never take first.

I just had a feeling about this little horse, a bit like the feelings I'd had on Miley way back at home in Ireland when I'd seen myself winning big races on him while we were kicking along the training tracks. No, for some reason, I just knew he would be the one to get me off the mark.

The race meet was very close to Bruce's farm in Pennsylvania, and we had only a few miles to go to get there. I invited Arabella, the girl I'd been dating at the time, to the race. We'd been seeing each other for a while and we were getting pretty serious. She accepted and I agreed to take her out to dinner as soon as I was paid for the win.

On the morning that Bruce and me were leaving to the track one of the chickens that Bruce kept at the barn crapped on my helmet from the rafters. I was about to wipe it off when Bruce started yelling, "Don't rub it off! It's good luck when that happens!"

Bruce really could make anything lucky in his own mind, be it a hat, a shirt or tie, so I left the chicken crap on my helmet and just smiled. "Who knows," I remember thinking to myself, "maybe he's right."

The race itself was not a super race; it was just a ten thousand dollar claimer and Apache Twist was not the favorite. There was another horse in the race whose jockey had started out about the same time as me and even though we were friends, I didn't want to finish second to him. I didn't consider him a better rider than me, he just seemed to get the breaks and really that is what the game is all about, being in the right place at the right time.

Apache was solid that day. He jumped great in behind and relaxed the way he knew how and the way I was now learning.

Three jumps from home this little fighter was still flying and I just knew he was a winner. The funny thing about it is that this is how he always ran; flying right up until the point he had to pass the last horse then that was when he would slow down and say "thanks for coming but the show is over."

Well, not today. We rolled down to the last fence just behind the favorite, and it was my old friend, who I was not going to lose to on this day. We landed safely, and I drove Apache with everything I had to get him up by a neck at the wire. I could feel his head rise as he was about to pass the other horse, and I knew he was thinking of putting on the breaks, but I yelled at him with all I had that on this day he was not going to finish second.

I'm not sure if it was my Irish accent, or the crazy sound of my voice, but he responded. He dropped his head down in front at the wire.

Apache Twist had gotten there, and in just under four minutes.

As we crossed the line, everything I'd worked so hard for over the past three years all seemed worth it; all the pain, the broken bones, the bad jobs; all of it just didn't seem to matter; I was a winner. I liked it and the feeling that came with it.

Winning your first real race, it's a feeling you never forget but also will never feel again. It's just never the same. There might be bigger and better races to win but there will only be one first win.

True to his word, Bruce paid me his percentage that week with my wages. It was the most money I'd held in my hand at one time in my life. All in all the win was worth fifteen hundred dollars to me, and I felt rich.

As promised, I took Arabella out to dinner and for about fifteen minutes I felt like I was on top of the world. The funny thing is that Arabella and me went our separate ways a few weeks later.

Following our brake up, I had a difficult time focusing on my work. Arabella and I had built up things in our heads and had dreamt of a future together, and suddenly it was gone.

We were two kids who were really in love. This was our first love, and it was our first heartbreak. I'd had enough. It seemed to me that as one door opened two were shut. It was the first time since I'd come to America that I felt alone and that I'd made a huge mistake in coming here.

For a reason I couldn't truly understand at the time, or admit to myself, I left Bruce's and the life I was making there and went to New York to drown my sorrows. I knew there were tons of Irish lads in New York and felt like I could fit in there.

Before leaving, I tried to explain myself to Bruce, and he actually understood. He didn't think I was right, but he knew about relationships good and bad and how we all deal with them in our own ways. As far as he was concerned, if I wanted to run off and hide, well that was my decision to make, and it was my shoulders that would have to carry the load that went with it.

I just didn't want to be around people and a world that reminded me of my ex-girlfriend. It seems so childish looking back; today, me and Arabella are friends and see each other all the time, but back then I would bump into her everywhere I went so I just left.

I suppose I was a child in many ways, but as with everything in life, things happen for a reason. I went to New York, galloped horses in the mornings, and worked in a deli near the track in the afternoons. Then, I would hit the pubs with the track lads at night, where we exchanged stories about the races we'd won.

In our minds, we were all champion jockeys, but I'm sure that more than half of the stories we shared were not true.

I did this for the next three to four months and really, it was starting to get old. I was twenty years old by now and had only ridden one winner that counted and I had no stories that mattered to me.

My story hadn't even started, and I knew it. I wanted more and knew it would be an uphill battle to get it, but I was ready and like I said, everything happens for a reason.

*M*y little boys.

6

Obsession and Loss

When I decided to return to riding in races, it really left me with no other option but to make it a success. Sure people go through life stopping and starting and some make it out okay, but for me I knew this was my last shot to get it right.

While in my self-imposed exile in New York, I'd often thought about the drive to the airport with my dad. I knew this was never what he wanted for me. I wasn't living either of our dreams by hiding myself away.

As would be the case throughout my life, just when I thought I was at my lowest, salvation was a

phone call away. This time trainer Toby Edwards tele-
phoned to offer me the opportunity of riding for him.

It was only through friends kicking me in the arse
that I decided to accept his offer.

Toby flew me down to ride Java to Go at Fox
Field. I really wasn't in the best of shape, physically or
mentally. We finished third and Toby ended up offering
me a job in Camden, South Carolina.

In time, I regained my form and confidence.

Later that fall, I rode my second winner for Bruce
Haynes, a trainer who later influenced my life. Like his
son Russell, Bruce became a good friend and in the years
to come, I looked to Bruce for advice.

In the coming months, I rode in a few races here
and there, but nothing special, not in my eyes anyway. I
often wondered if I was destined to ride decent horses in
decent races but never the big time.

I settled in and became the jockey I dreamed of
being as a boy.

A random thought or comment can lead to great
things. I'm not sure if anyone famous ever said that, but
they should have.

I was standing by a fence at the Montpelier steeplechase races in the fall of 2000 watching a stake's race.
Al Skywalker, one of the horses entered in the race, was
in the lead. Something about that little horse and how he
attacked the fences made me say aloud how much I
would love to ride him. Deidre Walsh was standing near
me and said she knew the trainer and would tell her if
she ever needed a rider to keep me in mind.

Time passed and then one day, while I was
sweeping the aisle in Toby's barn I got the call that
would change everything for me. "Is this Tom Foley?" a
woman's voice asked on the other end of the phone.

"It is." I answered.

"I was told you like my horse, Al Skywalker, and
I was wondering if I could book you to ride him in the
Carolina Cup."

I was hesitant, people play jokes all the time, and
I was sure I was having my leg pulled.

"Are you sure you have the right number?" I
asked. "I've only ridden a few winners, and the Carolina
Cup is a Grade One stake."

"I've got the right number. This is Jennifer Majette, Al Skywalker's trainer and co-owner, can you
come up and pop him over a few fences and we'll take it
from there."

Not sure if I would hear laughter and a "Gotta
Foley!" on the other end, I said "Sure."

It was Jennifer alright. We made arrangements for me to meet up with her and Al Skywalker a few days later.

When we met, one of the first things she said was, "Deidre told me you liked Al Skywalker. He needs a rider who will just go with him and not try to slow him down."

I grinned and said I could do that for sure and then I asked Jennifer about Al. She told me that he was a cast off, a failed flat horse who couldn't break his maiden running at the cheapest levels on the West Coast. He was sold for seven hundred dollars and the price of a van ride from California to North Carolina. He had won a few races over jumps, but like me, his form was far from consistent.

Dooley Adams, the champion jockey from the fifties was there too. He owned the horse with Jennifer. They showed me where to jump him and away Al and I rode.

What can I say? Al and I clicked, very simple. We just flew. He was so much fun to ride. It was awesome. I could tell from the start that he was special.

Al was the only horse Jennifer had in training so it was a big step up for her to try him in a Grade One with his form and an unproven jockey.

I remember telling one of the leading riders at the time that I was riding Al Skywalker in the Carolina Cup.

He laughed and muttered that "some people never learn."

He might have had a point, but everyone learned soon enough that Jennifer was right; Al galloped home the twelve-length winner of the Carolina Cup.

It was my third official win ever.

In the years that followed, Al Skywalker and I captured a number of the big hurdle stakes in this country and over the next four seasons, we even took Al to run at the biggest steeplechase venue in the world, Cheltenham in England.

Funny, but I look back at this period as really the point where I understood myself for the first time. I loved what I was doing and had found a way to make a decent living doing it. I'd learned from Mickey and Bruce how to care about horses and see them for what they are, the beautiful creatures that enabled me to make my living.

In my first full year of riding on a regular basis, I became the leading apprentice in the country for steeplechasing, think of it as rookie of the year, and had finished up as the third leading rider overall in the nation. It was a huge turn around from where I was the year before.

I promised myself that I would never run away from life again, and I told myself that no matter how tough things got I was going to keep pushing forward. Gregg Ryan would say it takes more courage to walk through life than to gallop down to a five-foot fence.

He was right.

I was about to be twenty-one, and my life was finally on track. I was winning races and meeting women. One of the women I met was named Krissy. We clicked right away. She was fun to be around and seemed to take everything in stride. She had grown up doing the horse shows and had since started exercising race horses. We worked in the same areas for a long time, but had never met until she came to a party at Gregg's after one of the race meets.

I knew right away that Krissy was different and like I said, we just clicked. I used to laugh at her because the reason she was galloping race horses was for the extra money to pay for board on her twenty-six-year-old ex-show horse. I would tell her she was crazy but she would just say, "Spring was good to me and now it's my turn to be good to her."

I admired this about Krissy. She had a good heart, and she loved Spring and the rest of her horses. You would think that we were a perfect fit. Funny thing is, we were, and it scared the crap out of me.

Since breaking up with Arabella, I had done nothing but focus my energy on my career. I had also remembered a "condition" that I'd come up with when I was a boy.

You see, I'd grown up in a country where people marry young and have large families, and there seemed to be no magic in their lives after that. I called it "Irish Farmer Syndrome", IFS for short. This was when a guy spent his whole life working the land and tending to his animals and then woke up one fine morning thinking, "Well, I've got land and a business, but I've got no family."

So out he would march and find a wife. Now, the first girl he found that wanted to drive on his tractor with him was selected, and they were married.

Wham bam, done and dusted.

In my mind, I'd come too far to start thinking about going down that path again.

No, I wasn't going to "expose" myself to IFS a second time. I had to stay true to the path I'd set for myself.

Even so, I knew that my feelings for Krissy were different. But, like I said, it scared me. I used every excuse I could think of to drive her away, but she still wanted to try and make things work.

I just couldn't do it. I was too young to stop doing the things I needed to reach the top, and in my mind, it was best to do it alone.

I now know that Krissy never wanted to get married, but the pressure I'd put on myself to succeed and the imaginary pressure that came with a relationship I just couldn't handle put me over the edge. I know she took it hard when we broke up, but all I wanted to be at this stage in my life was a champion jockey, and I was going to do everything I could to make that happen.

By the spring of 2002, I was back at Bruce Miller's where I was the go-to jockey. I was proud of the fact that in a couple of years, I'd come from a starting-out apprentice to being a first call jockey.

Things were different this time around. I'd won a lot of races, and Bruce liked how strong I was in a finish so he seemed to put a lot of trust in me and really the fact that I'd looked up to him so much in the beginning made this seem so much better, because if Bruce believed in me, then I must be doing okay.

Eddie Graham, Bruce's assistant, was still there. We became close friends and often went out to bars together.

Life was pretty much going in the right direction. I was winning and had slipped into a routine of racing and womanizing. It was any twenty-two-year-old's dream.

Towards the end of the year, I found myself in a position I didn't see coming, I met a woman named Kati at a party. She was a three-day event rider and to be honest, I was drawn to her fearlessness. It seemed strange to me to be around a woman who was that daring. Don't get me wrong, she was a beautiful girl, but it was her daring that set her apart from all the other beautiful girls.

From the very beginning, Kati and I had a turbulent relationship. For starters, she was a smoker and I hated that, as my dad smoked when I was a kid, and I'm sure it was a major factor in his heart attack. I'd sworn to myself that I would never date anyone who smoked, but then she just quit and I was fine with seeing how things went.

Coming off the 2002 racing season, I found myself able to relax. Being back at Bruce's helped as it smoothed the transition from apprentice champ into a proper professional jockey. I was also riding good horses which made me feel as if I didn't have to drive people away as I no longer saw them as a distraction.

At twenty-two years of age, I was comfortable enough with where my career stood to allow Kati into my life. Looking back, I should've seen that we were too similar for it to ever work. We were both stubborn, and determined, and passionate about what we were doing.

Kati and I broke up repeatedly and yet we still seemed to think that being together was a good idea. Our relationship soon took a dramatic turn when she called me one day while I was driving home from schooling young horses. We had had a fight that morning over me not being able to make some function with her as planned. I told her I had to do my job, but in her mind, I should have put it off so I could accompany her.

Maybe I should've, but I was still focused on being a champion jockey. Anyway, the phone rings and Kati tells me she's pregnant. Once again my life was changed by a phone call.

I was shocked to say the least.

I muttered out the "are you sure" and "how do you know" lines, but she was certain. The rest of the drive home was a blur.

Now for some reason, the Catholic in me rose up and I thought we needed to get married. Babies need a dad was my thinking and they should be born into a proper home.

We married, and in April of the following year, Kati gave birth to twin boys. I missed their birth by less than a day as they were born about seven weeks early and I'd been under contract to ride in Japan. I'd flown back the week before they were born to see her, and the doctors assured me that she would be fine until the next month, so I returned to Japan.

I would not have gone back, but I was booked to ride Gilded Age in the $1,750,000 Nakayama Grand Jump. Gilded Age was close to being the favorite and I'd just finished third on him in a million dollar race a month before, so with the babies on the way it made sense to go for a huge pay out.

I finished fourth in the Nakayama; even so, in the months that followed, Kati and I used some of the money I earned in Japan to put a down payment on a house. We lived there for a while and later sold the place and bought a farmhouse.

Being a dad to the twins came naturally to me; I liked it and even though Kati and I had rushed into marriage, we actually got along. We soon had another little boy. We named him Kieran after my friend who by this point had passed away.

While I was in Japan, Al Skywalker had run twice. He had finished a distant third in a four horse race and was last in his other start. Jennifer called and asked if I would ride him in the Marcellus Frost Grade

Three hurdle at the Iroquois Race Meet in Nashville, Tennesee. I gladly accepted.

It was a tough race and Al was not the favorite going in especially since he had given weight to all his competition.

Al and I went to the front as usual and Al put on a display of jumping I will never forget. Everytime he got close to the wings, he accelerated and took off. He really was pure magic.

Climbing the hill the last time, I could feel the closing pack crowding in around us. They got close, but they never passed Al. He saw the final two fences and just took off. He won as he pleased. I was delighted, and I punched the air as we passed the finish line.

I was happy to be reunited with my favorite horse and doing what we do best, winning.

Someone asked me once if I had to ride a horse into battle, which one I would pick. It would always be Al. He really was a warhorse.

When we reached the winner's circle I noticed that Jennifer was crying. She always got emotional, but this was different. When I weighed in and the pictures were taken, she came up and hugged me. "That's it," she said, "he has done enough. He deserves to go out a champ."

The horse was eleven years old and had six-hundred-thousand dollars in the bank; he had earned his retirement. I was sad and happy with her decision. He had earned his right to go out and just be a horse. I admired Jennifer's love for him to stop when she did. Sure, there were more races for him to win, but why let him fall down the ladder? We all think of Muhammad Ali in his prime and choose to forget how his career ended. Jennifer didn't want that for Al.

Al still lives in Southern Pines, North Carolina, and is fat and happy in his retirement. Jennifer never got anymore horses. Now she just takes care of her champion.

Following Al's retirement, I continued riding a lot of nice horses, but there had been magic with Al, and when he was no longer there I missed him.

As things started to slow a bit for me, Kati and I started training a few horses. I'd been in the country for eight years: I'd won races; I'd won money, and I'd won championships. It seemed like the next logical step would be to stop and concentrate on training fulltime. With the kids, it would be smarter, and it was creeping into my head that it was time to do what was right for them, but a part of me couldn't let racing go – couldn't let winning go.

When we start out anything we really are innocent, that goes for nearly everything in life. We come into the world innocent and as we move on we change and maybe we just don't see things the same. Now that might not be all that bad, but for me, looking back, I see the change that led the innocent kid who just wanted to be a jockey and be with horses into becoming a person consumed with winning.

I really didn't understand winning when I started out. I mean how could I? Sure, I dreamed about it, but I had no idea what it meant. In my mind, it was just about being the first one past the post and the thrill of it alone was enough. The innocence disappeared when I felt on top for the first time. It was probably greater because I had struggled for so long to feel it.

It might be different for people who start out winning. It happens. Kids get lucky and they get live mounts thrown at them and really winning is all they know; not so for me. When I finally found it, winning felt good, and I wanted to experience that feeling more and more. During the off-season, I would travel to New Zealand, Japan and England, anywhere and everywhere to ride a winner.

Simply put, I was addicted to winning.

Whenever I got the chance to ride, I would go. Kati took the brunt of this obsession. She wanted a husband who was a stable father figure; a man who'd stay at home with her and the kids, but I still had the burning in me to win. I justified leaving by telling myself that at this age the kids needed their mommy more than me.

The thing is that it was never about the money, it was all about the winning. Winning was a thrill that I couldn't seem to rid my body from wanting and I pursued it to a point where I eventually drove my wife with no option but to leave. I never saw the pain I was causing her as all I thought about was the fact that she was holding me back.

I also didn't see how my attitude towards horses was changing yet again from one of love and compassion to seeing them as nothing more than the tools I needed to win races. Maybe that is why I did so well in Japan. The Japanese saw me as a super aggressive rider, and during my three month contract there I rode in a number of big races and won them. They liked my do or die attitude, and I liked the winning, and I must admit, the money I was making.

I was nearly always on my own while I was in Japan. I just had my interpreter with me on race days so it became easy to mimic their attitude towards horses; they were nothing more than tools used for entertainment and for winning.

Racing in Japan was so regimental that even the people that surrounded me seemed to have little personality. It seeped through to the horses; it was like an army of robots with no emotions. Just people and animals who did their jobs until it was time to move on, be it retirement for the grooms or riders, or the next stop for the horses. Back then, I didn't know about the *usual* next stop for a horse. It was only when I read about Ferdinand much later that it all made sense to me.

Ferdinand was a race horse who had won the 1986 Kentucky Derby and the 1987 Breeders' Cup Classic. He also won the 1987 Eclipse Award for Horse of the Year. He entered stud in 1989 and in 1994 was sold to a breeding farm in Japan. When he failed to live up to expectations, in 2002, he was sent to slaughter with no fanfare or notice to his previous owners in America. He likely became pet food or steaks for human consumption.

Yes, Ferdinand had been a great race horse who really battled in his races. He had talent and a heart to match; to think where that heart ended up is just sickening and sad.

If I'd been myself at the time, or the person I am today, maybe I would've seen it or known what lay in store for horses that didn't win, but I didn't.

To be honest maybe you just have to see enough of everything before you're either willing to understand it or confront it, I was in a place back then where I could do neither.

When I returned to America, the aggression and drive I'd used to make it in Japan flowed into a great year for me in the States. I was winning left and right and was feeding the addiction that had taken over my mind. Perhaps you can justify bad things or ignore them because you're blinded by winning. Who knows?

All I knew was I liked winning and did not want to go back to struggling. I'd been there before, and not just in my early days in America, but at home as a child. My mam and dad had done their best and it's not like we starved, but they had to work hard to provide for us, there were plenty of times when we went without because what we wanted was just not necessary.

But by now, I had a convertible and nice clothes; all the trappings I felt were necessary for me. Having kids contributed to my feelings of wanting to do more than just get by. After they arrived, I wanted the same for them that I now had and winning was my means of providing it all. It was the best of both worlds. I got to win, and I had a family who had it all.

My feelings for the racing game eventually got between Kati and me. We would fight over it, and finally one day when I was leaving to go racing, Kati reached the end of her rope. "Is this what you want," she yelled at me, "to keep riding until you kill yourself and the kids are left with no father?" Her daring spirit had been snuffed out by the feelings of protection a mother has for her young kids and husband. She had had enough, and really it's hard for me to blame her.

"I hope you die like your friend," she shouted as I kept walking, "and I never see you again!"

She was talking about Kieran, my friend who we had named our youngest son after.

To hear her say this rocked me to the core.

I went and rode Shady for Bruce. It was a three-hour drive to the track. Along the way, I tried to understand why Kati had said those things to me, but I couldn't.

Looking at it now, I can understand her not wanting to be left alone, but at the time it hurt, and it started to drive a wedge between us.

We held it together for about seven more months, but by then we just couldn't do it anymore. We had grown apart, and there was just too much bitterness to keep putting the kids through it. I don't care how young kids are they know when their parents are not getting along and they don't deserve the fighting.

Kati went back to her parents in Minnesota with the boys, and I stayed in the big farmhouse we had bought the year before. She soon filed for divorce and when the time came I signed the papers.

DIVORCE: I even feel funny writing it. I'd learned from the time I was a young boy that divorce was unacceptable and really when it happened to me it was the first time I'd thought about how I might look to people at home or at least my family. I was brought up Catholic, and well, the funny thing is, that Catholics don't get divorced.

I remember talking to mam and dad about it. They were trying to hide it from people as if it was such a shame that people knew. Sure it was fine to talk about divorce in America; after all, everyone did it over here, but not at home, not in Ireland.

It hurt to feel that they were ashamed of me. I know now that they were not, but at the time, it was strange, as none of us really knew how to deal with it. I remember my mother telling me that I had to tell my grandmother, as she just couldn't do it. Well, I did, and my seventy-nine-year-old grandmother was the first to make me feel normal about it. "It happened child," she said to me, "you had to do what was best for you."

I'm not sure if it was what was best for me, but the fact that my grandmother understood enabled me to relax and not feel like a loser.

We've all heard about Catholic guilt. Believe me it's real. You don't need to go to church every Sunday to know it; it hits you when you fail in the eyes of the faith that surrounded you as a child. Maybe divorce was a way of getting me to identify again with the country I'd left so many years ago. I don't know, but I thought about it a lot.

*I*t was during the months that I was alone in the house that I hit the low that started me down the road to switching over to riding on the flat, and learning about flipping.

People might think that you're crazy when you say a house talks to you. Well, mine did, or maybe it was the fact that it was so quiet that it drove me nuts. I would try to sleep at night, but it was so quiet that I couldn't. I was so used to hearing the kids making noise. The baby monitor that we used for Kieran was still plugged in and at times, I would find myself looking at it, praying that I would hear a noise from the kids at the other end. It never happened.

I would walk around the house and walk into their old room and look at the big stuffed toys that my ex-wife had left behind as she couldn't fit them in when she packed up.

I started taking Nyquil to try and sleep. It worked for a while, but I still walked around the house at night. Sometimes I would wake up in the morning in the kids' room amongst their old stuffed toys. It was getting to me; I had to get out of there. I'd messed up my marriage by my unwillingness to stop doing what I felt had made me, and now it seemed like my only option was to continue riding.

I didn't want to be around the steeplechase world as there were always too many questions that I didn't feel like answering, so flat racing seemed like the way to go. Besides, I now had three kids and an ex-wife to support so I made the decision to lose the weight and once again work until I got to a point where I felt I was a success.

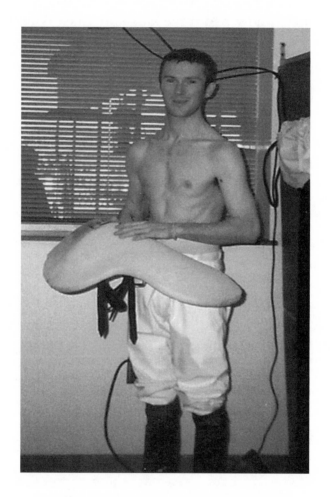

*A*t one hundred and nine pounds.

7

The Lost Years

A few friends knew of my decision to switch from steeplechasing to flat racing. One of them, Ed Saxton, the farm manager for the late George Steinbrenner, invited me to Tampa Bay Downs where he promised to introduce me to trainers. Ed was a likable fellow so people were always keen to help him out, even if it meant giving someone a shot to ride based solely on his recommendation.

I soon rode my first winner and before long, I was gaining experience by riding on a steady basis.

Flat racing differed greatly from steeplechasing. For example, I found it difficult to get use to the starting gate as we didn't have one in jumping. I couldn't miss a beat at the gate as one mistake cost me so many lengths that were hard to make up during a race, especially when I wasn't riding the best horses.

It was hard to go from doing well at a sport to being the low man on the totem pole. Sure, I'd taken the time to train as a flat jockey and I copied what I saw the other jocks doing, but I was still having a rough time. There was one veteran rider who took me under his wing. His name was Vernon Bush. He was a good guy and a good rider. He helped me out with the gate and spent a lot of time trying to get me to stay low in the saddle.

To be honest, I looked like a bloody beacon sticking straight up in the air. As a jump rider, you sit up looking for the next jump as you're racing, but on the flat it's all about aerodynamics and getting rid of wind resistance. Vernon worked and worked with me until I finally started looking more in uniform with the other riders.

My natural body weight was around one-hundred-and-forty pounds, but by the time I reported to Tampa Bay, I'd lost twenty-five pounds by dieting and trying to do all the right things, but it was so bloody hard to keep it up.

One of the methods I used to control my weight was sitting in what we called "the box." To be honest, the experience was sheer hell. Think of the sauna at your local gym and then crank it up twenty-five or so degrees and you can get an idea of what it was like.

Before going in I would cover my body in baby oil to block the pours so when it got really hot my body would just pop and the weight would pour off. At first, I couldn't sit in there for more than twenty minutes, but in time, I got used to it and could sit in it for hours.

It was at this time that the event I wrote about at the beginning of this book took place. I went to dinner with some jockeys and learned about the art of flipping.

After that night, one of the jocks must've felt some regret in telling me about flipping because in the weeks that followed he kept warning me about how bad flipping was for me: "From your teeth, to your stomach and heart, to your mind," he would say, "flipping fucks them all up."

I told him that I didn't flip and that I was not willing to pay the price that would have to be paid.

I was lying. I knew about all the dangers that came with flipping, but I was willing to pay the price, and it wasn't just because I wanted to win. It was because at this point in my life, I just didn't care. The faster I got to where I was going was fine with me and to hell with the consequences.

Besides, I didn't want this jockey or anyone else knowing about my flipping for the same reason that I never talked about my divorce; it was my business and it was my shame to hide.

Flat racing made it easy for me to keep my secrets and to bury my head in the sand and disappear. Gregg would tell me it was not the right path, that there was no quick fix, but I wasn't listening and just kept on down the road of self-destruction.

In many ways I was hiding from myself as well; I knew that, but like anything else I had to be willing to face my problems in order to fix them and that wasn't something I was interested in doing.

I started making my living by volunteering to ride the horses others wouldn't dare ride. It was easy, because after losing my boys there really wasn't much a crazy or sore horse could do to hurt me.

Physical pain was nothing in comparison to the pain I felt inside. I missed my boys and the adrenaline rush from knowing the added danger seemed the best way to quiet the demons I lived with on a daily basis.

I soon became conscious of my appearance and my resemblance to a skeleton. I started staying away from people. The most shameful thing to develop, however, was the loss of contact with my kids. I didn't want them seeing me. Somewhere along the way, I fell into the belief that by sending them money and calling everyday that it counted as being a dad, but as the weight came off the distance between my kids and me grew larger.

In the years to come, I went from daddy to Tom, and eventually one night when I asked one of the twins if he missed his dad he said, "My daddy's name is Charlie and he's right here." My ex-wife, Kati, had remarried and Charlie was the name of her new husband.

It was my fault. I'd let the distance grow. Being paranoid about putting on weight if I stepped outside my routine and being embarrassed by the way I looked had kept me away from them, and now I was more of a stranger than a dad.

Looking back, I can't understand or defend my thinking, but it happened. My marriage, while I will not call it bad, was at least mismatched; two people who didn't know what they were getting into and were really unaware of each other's dreams and goals in life. Love in itself is sometimes not enough to make things work. Kati and I did create three beautiful boys and for that I will always be grateful, as I love them with all my heart.

Like love, I thought that riding horses would be simple, but in the flat racing world, I discovered that it wasn't. From the weights, to the drugs, to the horses patched together for one last race, I found that the racing game was not simple, and that was the part that just sucked the life out of me.

Today, I can look at my time in Florida as a major turning point in my life. It's easy to understand it now, but at the time I was a lost soul looking for a place to hide. I'd given up a marriage for a career that I had left behind and now I was lost. When you torture yourself you get to know the boundaries and limits that you can push your body to. It's almost like selling your soul to play the game by the damage you do to yourself. You can't take it back, and it will linger with you forever.

I see it now, and trust me, on most days I feel the toll that flipping took on my body. Even today, I still get dizzy or pains from the ulcers caused by my diet or lack of one.

Flat racing was a far different sport than the one I was used to. Sure, any normal person would say that the difference between jumping and flat racing was that in one, horses ran over jumps and in the other, they ran on the flat, and that's it.

But, I can tell you that jumping is much different as you just can't patch a horse together and expect him to race over jumps and still win, and as there is not that much racing over jumps in America, owners want to win, and trainers know they can't win if they are running sore horses. So really, in steeplechasing you never race a horse that's not ready.

For me to go from the steeplechase world where people seemed to at least care that the horses they ran were sound, to a world where horses were held together with chemicals was tough. In the beginning, I noticed it a lot and wondered if I'd made the right choice by switching to flat racing.

I thought about leaving, running away, but I had nowhere to go, no place to hide.

I'd come from riding favorites in steeplechases to riding thirty-to-one long shots in low level claimers. It was on those animals that I realized what exactly I was sitting on. It wasn't easy to face riding those types of horses everyday. A lot of them hit the ground like a ton of bricks when they moved, and others were so sore that they acted up and were unruly as they were trying to say how much it hurt them to be put through the ordeal of running every day.

It was hard to see this at first, but as I was so miserable in my own life I just went along with it and did what I had to do to survive and keep making money for the kids.

After a while, the shock of seeing these animals in the state they were in left me, and it became normal.

I went from expecting sound and happy horses to knowing I would be riding sore and grumpy ones, but I never cared how rough they were or how much they acted up. I would ride them if there was no one else or if someone refused to ride them. Simply put, I'd gone from shocked to no concern in just a few weeks. It just flowed over me, and I was gone. My conscience had shut off, and everything was normal in my mind.

I lost track of the times I was on my way to post on a hot favorite and as soon as he started to move in the warm up, I knew that he wasn't right. Sometimes it was the way a horse hit the ground, and I felt a dramatic unevenness in his gate or he was washed out and getting seaty and overheated.

Maybe a horse I was riding had some physical problem and was in pain, but instead of being given time to heal the trainer decided to inject the animal with pain medication so he could make it through a race; anything to keep an owner happy.

The trainer knew his horse wasn't one-hundred percent and maybe the owner did too, but often times a rider was unaware of the fact. Add all of this up by ten horses in a race, and it amounts to forty legs that may have some problems, problems that were treated with painkillers. These horses were hitting the ground at thirty-five miles an hour, now the risk factor had risen dramatically. It would only take one leg to go and a horse to fail in order for the domino effect to begin. In such close quarters, there was no escape or place to hide. If a horse dropped in front of you going that fast, odds were you were going down as well. It really took very little for this to happen.

There were drugs and steroids for all manner of things, painkillers and blocker shots to make horses more aggressive and ones to calm them down. We have all seen the movies where the football player gets injured and begs the doctor to shoot him up so he can make one more play to help win the game. It was the same thing here, except the horse never asked for the shot. The injection was just given, and they were sent out to try and win.

Aside from being raced when they were not ready, when a horse was moved from one trainer to another these guys didn't share information with each other pertaining to the horse. So when the new guy got a horse, he would go in with his own set of needles to fix all the problems the horse had according to his opinion, a jab here a jab there and on and on it went.

So how did I calculate risk?

The answer is I couldn't. As a rider I just had to rely on what I felt from the horse and his movement. I can't begin to count the number of times I worked a sore horse in the morning and reported it to the horse's trainer only to hear him say, "Don't worry jock, he'll be a hundred percent on race day."

Yes, I got used to things. It's hard to write this now as I believe I did my fair share of damage to the animals I love. My only defense is that I was doing equal damage to myself so I wasn't mentally there for either of us.

I took sleeping pills to forget about life and horses and to quelch the headaches and the dizzy spells. In all, I lost three years of my life by sleeping my way through the times when riding no longer brought me the peace I'd dreamed and hoped for since I was a little boy.

I started to ask myself who the hell I was and how I'd gotten to this point in life; a life where I didn't recognize my face in the mirror. Hell, I'd gone from one hundred and forty pounds to one hundred and nine. I had obviously changed physically but had never cared enough to notice it. I had simply shut myself off from thinking about it and kept pressing on, to where, I wasn't sure. Life just seemed to flow from one track to the next, and I just went along with it.

I also wondered how I was going to get back to a point in my life where I was happy and how I could be a part of my little boys' lives.

Maybe in the years to come, when they're older, and they read this, maybe they'll understand their dad for the man he was and for the man he hoped to become. Maybe then they'll understand that in my mind I was doing what I thought was right.

*M*entally and physically; I knew the end was near.

8

A Time for Change

As the work at Tampa Bay Downs ended, I received an offer to ride in California. I accepted and soon after my arrival found that it too was a different world. The horses seemed sounder and the trainers welcoming. I immediately got opportunities from established trainers to ride and really it was a huge lift in spirit to even be there.

The purses on the West Coast were larger and the atmosphere at Hollywood Park suited me perfectly. Even so, my mind was still not completely there. I was just four months from my kids moving away and that was driving me crazy. I wasn't sleeping and with trying to keep my weight down, I was a walking semi-functioning wreck.

One trainer I was riding for was a very interesting man, and he seemed easy to talk to. His name was Vladimir Cerin. I know now that he could see that I was troubled. He tried to get me to talk about what was bothering me. I told him a bit about my divorce and how the whole situation with the kids was getting to me.

Vladimir was good to talk to. His wife had passed away in an accident. He told me how losing his best friend in the whole world had rocked him, and he would never find that again. He told me that his life and mind were set, but that I still had the option of doing something about my life and my way of thinking.

I knew he was right, but I also knew that it was far easier said than done.

I stayed at Hollywood Park for three months or so. I tried to get going, but with the small fields and strong pool of jockeys, it was a struggle to get on the better horses.

There was also the expense of living in Southern California. It was bloody expensive. I knew that there was no way that I was going to be able to pay for the kids and stay afloat.

I was struggling, and I needed to make a change. I decided to head back to the east coast to ride at Charlestown.

One morning, I told Vladimir about my plans and the fact that I wasn't making it financially. I told him I needed to go where I could make a better living and take care of my boys. He told me people with talent would always find their place and calling, if they were not afraid to look.

He knew things were not going great at that time and wanted to help. He asked me if I needed some money for the cross-country drive.

I accepted his offer and told him that I would pay him back as soon as I rode a winner or two.

I drove the three thousand miles with nothing on my mind but getting back to the east coast; back to Charlestown; back to the places I knew were calling me.

It was time to settle down to just being a work-man jockey and trying to make a living doing one of the few things I knew how to do, win.

I drove day and night, until at last, I saw Charlesown in the distance, I'd made it. Now all I needed was to find horses to ride. I did, and after a while, I began to settle down to a daily routine at the track.

It's hard to describe a day in the life of a jockey at a small track; you get to work at six with your agent and hustle around getting on horses for different trainers all morning. There is no guarantee that you'll be riding on any given race day; nothing in racing is guaranteed.

It is all about what have you done for me lately and that's it.

On most mornings, I would work ten or more horses and then head off to ride at Laurel before returning at night to ride at Charlestown.

My life consisted of either sitting on a horse, a car seat or in a bloody sauna. Yes, weight and keeping it down was always on my mind; always with me. The worst at Charlestown was during winter racing when we ran at night in fifteen-degree weather. It was torture going out into that cold after sitting in the box.

After a few years of riding at Charlestown, fear slowly started creeping into my mind, but not in the way you might think. I'd become familiar with all of the characters on and off the track. During morning workouts, I would see a variety of people that made up the patch work quilt that is a race track.

Fear for me was ending up like the people I saw in the mornings; guys that never made it as race riders; guys who had turned to galloping horses in the mornings to make a living; guys who were bitter at the hand life had dealt them, and who hated their jobs and the horses they rode.

I would see them every morning going by, and as soon as a horse made the slightest move they didn't approve of they were kicking the horse and shouting names: "I'll teach you motherfucker!" This saying should be on bumper stickers for these people. They bully horses just to make themselves feel in control and important.

I saw, and more often than not, heard these people every morning. It started to creep into my mind that I could end up like them: Scared, bitter and miserable.

"Is that what lay ahead?"

Not for me, I kept telling myself, but as I was becoming aware of this, I also had no real plan as to how to avoid it.

It was about this time that I found that blood in the toilet and my valet and I had agreed that I would see a doctor. I never did, and now my body seemed to be reaching the end.

It was getting harder and harder to keep my weight in check by simply flipping and taking handfuls of laxatives.

To combat my loosing battle, I spent long hours in the box. The torture that I was putting my body through could only last for so long; something had to give.

All these things were adding up, but, for some reason I kept pushing through. A few winners kept me motivated, and to be honest, I was enjoying the best year of my flat racing career in regards to winners. The only problem was I wasn't enjoying it.

I was miserable because of my diet and just seeing and riding these crippled horses was starting to get to me.

I thought about what Gregg had said to me long ago, "Is that the man you want to be?"

I was faced with a serious moral dilemma, especially when I was on my way to post and I knew the horse I was riding wasn't sound enough for what he was being made to do. I knew if I went to the vet and tried to get the animal scratched, it would get back to the trainer, and it would cost me mounts, and if I refused a ride, a trainer could always find someone else to take it.

All of a sudden, I would be branded a "chicken" and nobody would use me so, in reality, my hands were tied, and unless I wished to have no work at all, then I just had to shut up and do the best I could.

Now, not everything was bad at the track. There were good trainers and owners and very good riders who just didn't get the credit or results they deserved.

Frank Light was one such trainer that I came to admire. For instance, he booked me to ride his horse; a horse that was coming back after a long layoff. Light had heard that I was honest and would try hard for him so he offered me the ride.

When we met in the paddock he said, "Jock, don't mind the layoff. He needed some time, and we gave it to him. There isn't anything wrong with him."

I'd heard this speech tons of times but for some reason the way Light said it I believed him.

More often than not, however, the trainers at Charlestown sounded the same as those I'd encountered over my career. All of them always said the same thing, "This one can't get beat jock."

I can't count the number of times I heard a trainer say that. Picture yourself on a cold night in a paddock and some trainer telling you how it was such a waste of time for the other runners to show up, as his horse would win for the fun of it.

I heard this story night after night and so did every other jock in the paddock. There can only be one winner to every race, so when it was over, all but one of the guys in the race was going to have to explain to a trainer what had happened.

When I lost, I often knew why. I would talk to trainers in order to help them understand a loss. Some of them were grateful for the advice, but most saw the loss as my fault and felt as if they would win the next time as long as they hired a different jockey.

Their attitude toward me didn't bother me. If they didn't want to better their chances of having their horse win the next time out, that was their decision, not mine. I could care less.

I had changed so much from the once happy kid who just wanted to be a jockey to a drone who just went about his business and did his part then moved on, there was no love or passion anymore. I was just doing what I had to do to get by.

The funny thing about it though, was that at the time, I never realized it. I was so busy thinking about me and feeling sorry for myself that I thought of little else.

That's the way it was, but it was all about to change.

I was riding a filly one Sunday at Charlestown, and for me, it was a typical day. Nothing on the card stood out as a sure winner, but for the most part my horses all looked like decent mounts, with one exception, I was named on a filly that was having her eighteenth start in a maiden race. A maiden race is for horses that have yet to win a race so if a horse is still running in maidens after eighteen starts, well, it may be a sign that racing is not the animal's game.

This filly had a few decent starts way back and had managed to hit the boards a few times, but as time went on she had gotten worse. Her recent starts had been dismal. She'd acted up during post parades and had been unruly in getting into the gate.

Maybe the best part of racing is the fact that things change so much and you never know what is going to happen. If you're lucky you get to ride for good trainers that know their horses' talent level and have them placed in the right position to get the best results. You win; you lose and if all goes to plan, at least you come home safe, but as with anything in life things don't always go according to plan.

I smiled as I read this filly's form. I mean, Stevie Wonder himself could've seen that she didn't like her job. When horses start out okay and then get worse and eventually unruly, they are trying to tell someone that they are either hurting or really don't want to be doing this anymore.

Anyway, I made my way out to the paddock to see my trusty mount and meet her trainer. The first thing I saw was this washed out chestnut mare with sweat dripping everywhere and eyes bugging out of her head telling me that she would love to be anywhere but here. I marched over to the trainer to find out just how he expected me to get this fine steed to the winner's circle.

Now, you will have to work with me here as for some reason my typewriter will not let me type in a wannabe "Tony Soprano accent" so you'll just have to add that in for yourself.

The first thing the trainer told me was "jock, she's a little nervous."

"Thanks genius," I thought to myself. "I had that part figured out."

Then the trainer said, "Don't mind her last few races as the jocks didn't listen, and it was not the filly's fault that she lost. She is much better than her form suggests."

"Okay," I thought to myself, "I'm sure that the last few jocks who rode her were suicidal; they had gotten her wound up in the post parade and then had tried to get her acting bad in the gate just for fun."

The trainer then added, "Don't try and rush her early as she will flip her palate and stop."

A palate is part of a horse's airway system, and if they are nervous or excited it can flip and slow down the amount of air the horse can take in; therefore, slowing it down.

Now all of these things I was hearing were just to let me know that whatever I did I was going to get beat, and it would all be my fault. Nervous filly, bad wind problems, try and relax her the best I can: Okay, I got it!

Now, just as the trainer threw me up on the filly, this "Soprano-wanna-be" says, "Oh jock, remember she needs the lead, because if the dirt hits her in the face she'll stop and the game's over."

For those of you that understand horses and their inner workings and delicate minds this makes no sense, but with all respect, let me explain it a little for those of you who don't.

This was a maiden race of five thousand dollars, which is the lowest level there is at Charlestown and the race is run over the minimum distance of 4.5 furlongs, which is as short as it gets in most places. So for me to try and get this filly to relax and help her keep her breathing under control, yet make sure she gets the lead out of the gate over the minimum distance, is just pure nonsense.

She was a ball of nerves, and as we neared the post she was getting worse. Think of a spring all wound up tight just waiting to explode, and you may get an idea of what I was sitting on. She was sweating and running in every direction she could in order to get away from the pony leading her to the gate. Basically, she was doing all the things we don't want horses doing on their way to the start.

My mount was the number one horse so we were the first to approach the gate. Just as we were about to go in this poor girl boiled over. She reared up and flipped over. I was lucky in that she threw me far enough away from her that she didn't land on me. The poor thing got up fast and bolted off around the track. She was wild and the outriders tried catching her and did so only after she had made three solo trips around the track.

After she was finally caught and scratched from the race, I made my way back to the jock's room. Right as I got there her bewildered trainer, who was walking that fine line between confusion and anger, asked me what had happened. "She has never done that before," the trainer stammerd.

"I don't know boss," I said shaking my head and thinking about that poor filly, "it must've been me."

For all the good trainers that do the right thing by their horses and their jocks, there will always be a few who got their license from tokens on a cereal box. Some days all I could do was laugh; it really is a funny old game.

After this incident, I realized that animals like these were better off with me on them because I wouldn't push them to a point that it would break them down.

In my mind, I was looking after them, but really, it wasn't my job to look after them, that was the job of their owners and trainers. But nobody wanted to step up and do it, so despite the fact that I looked at them as a meal ticket, I was starting to gain back my old feelings for horses.

No, for them it was easier to just run the horse and if things didn't go right just blame the jockey and try again. Now, the trainer couldn't blame himself as it would cause him to lose the horse and also the day money the owner paid him and of course it was not the owner's fault when a horse broke down so it all fell on the shoulders of the jockey.

Things were starting to add up in my mind, and I knew I was close to the edge. Of what, I really didn't know, but something was going to have to give. I started to prepare for what I knew was coming. My body and mind were in a state of serious disrepair, and there was nothing I could do about it.

I knew I didn't want to end up broken down and scared, making my living exercising the animals that were in that exact same boat. The fear of that existence and becoming *that guy* was driving me in another direction.

But, for all the suffering horses, the hard falls and the broken bones I'd suffered over the years, there was one brush with near disaster that made me look up and take stock of the life I'd created for myself.

I rode at Laurel on this particular day. It was a card filled with nothing impressive. Afterwards, I drove to Charlestown for one ride that night in the seventh race, I liked the horse and at least on paper he had a serious shot of winning. I'd ridden him a few times in the past. He was bad in the gate, but usually ran a decent race once the gates were open. He was being dropped in to a four thousand dollar claimer, which in this area is as low as you can go; I thought he should be able to get the job done.

To be honest, he was a perfect cliché for horses at a small track. He was once running well at the larger places and either through injury or bad luck had fallen down the ladder to be running at this current level.

Like I said, I'd ridden him a few times and really wasn't worried about his antics in the gate. We broke well and managed to stay with the leaders.

As we neared the quarter pole, I was just about to split the leaders and make my bid for the wire when I heard the snap that all jockeys dread. To picture this imagine driving down the highway going seventy-five and looking over and seeing one of your tires flying by; it's that feeling at you going from being in control to trying to avoid a wreck.

I held the reigns tighter. Most of the time when horses snap a knee they will fall, but this classy old warrior did all he could to keep us both from hitting the ground. He knew he was done, but he didn't want to take me with him.

Experience told me to hold up the horse's head and to keep him on his feet if I could. As a jock it was your job to win and push the envelope, but it was also your job to protect the guys you rode with.

This classy old brute fought as hard as I did, and we got pulled up.

Over the years I'd had so many close calls, but I'd never had a "life flashing before your eyes" experience, but right as this was happening all I could hear was my son saying, "My daddy's name is Charlie," over and over.

I jumped off this horse, and as I pulled him up I held the reins. Adrenaline and medication was pumping through his system so I had to keep him from moving to limit any further damage.

As I waited for help, I stared into this warrior's eyes; we both knew his fate.

Suddenly, something in me awoke. My son's words rang in my ears, but all around me, the world was quiet. It was just this beautiful beast and me and as I looked into his eyes I thought about the horses I'd ridden over my career. I also thought about what Eddie Graham had said to me years before about how I just didn't get it; "It's not about you; it's about them."

He was right, and as I realized that I was staring at my reflection in this horse's eyes I understood that Eddie's words not only held true to horses, but that they also held true to my boys and my life. It wasn't about me; and it wasn't about me walking around feeling sorry for myself. It was about living and doing the best I could.

This revelation all happened in a matter of seconds, but for the life of me it felt like hours.

After about twenty seconds, my valet, Rickey Smallwood, arrived followed by the horse's groom and the state vet.

"You had me swearing boy," Rickey yelled, "I was worried about you!"

Somehow, I managed to say that it was all good, that I was still kicking.

I pulled off my tack and gave that warrior one last pat on the neck. I watched as he was loaded on the horse ambulance. From here, his fate was simple; a quick van ride off the track and the shot of pink juice to put him to sleep. We knew what lay in store for him, but we also knew the part he'd played in making sure our fates were not similar.

As Rickey and I turned to walk away from the scene, I heard one of the trainers in the group say, "It isn't so bad, we needed to make room for some better horses anyway."

At the start of the race, or even if we had finished the race, I wouldn't have given his comment a second thought, and sadly enough, I probably would've agreed with him.

But, something in me had changed; I knew that the Thomas Foley that had started the race had died and that the new Thomas Foley was ready to start living once again; ready to recapture the passion he had for the sport and the animals he had so loved as a boy.

I was furious! How could this prick say that? I wanted to take a swing at the guy. I mean this horse had stayed on his feet even though he was done for and kept me from a trip to the hospital or worse and all this trainer could say was he needed room for better horses. If Rickey hadn't grabbed me I'm sure I would've been in trouble for beating the ignorant fool with my whip. How could he be so callous?

It was eleven o'clock at night, but I needed a cold shower in the jockeys' quarters just to calm down. I knew how long those seconds of struggle felt like and how brave that horse had been; why, why, I thought to myself, couldn't the trainer?

I got home and still couldn't calm down. I had to be on the road at four in the morning so a few sleeping pills were out of the question. I was in a place I feared, alone with my own thoughts: "My daddy's name is Charlie," "It's probably for the best, as we need room for better horses."

How had it come to this; a stranger to my own kids, and riding for people who didn't give a damn about horses and jockeys.

My years of abusing sleeping pills and flipping were catching up with me.

I'd done it to myself, and as I sat there alone, I wondered why, and for what.

If I live a thousand years, nobody will ever convince me that the horse that saved my life that night didn't look at me as if to say I needed to change my life, as well as do something for the men and beasts that play this game every day and every night around this country.

He was right and I knew it. I'd seen it all so clearly, but like I said before, some things are much easier said than done.

*M*e and John Malkovich during the filming of
Walt Disney Studios' feature film *Secretariat*.

9

Being Tom Foley

I knew that I needed a break from racing. I needed time to take a long hard look at myself and to understand my place in this world. I also knew that I couldn't afford to stop racing. I needed the money to live on and to send to my boys.

Given the reality of my situation, I tried to change my life; tried to stop flipping and taking sleeping pills, but I couldn't. I was stuck and with each passing day my experience with that warrior in Charlestown became a distant memory.

On my days off, I spent some time with a good friend of mine, Russell Haynes, who at the time was a steeplechase jockey and later a bloodstock agent. I enjoyed getting away from my life on the track by spending time at the Haynes' place; a little farm hidden down in a valley on a mountain just outside Bristol, Tennessee.

I found peace and quiet there and enjoyed watching the relationship shared between Russell, his brother and their dad, Bruce, a horse trainer for whom I often rode horses.

On one particular night at the farm, Russell asked if anyone wanted some moonshine?

Russell and his roommate from college, Vann, were holding two jugs of the stuff and offering it to a room that included Russell's cousin, David and Russell's brother, Will, as well as Bruce. Passing this stuff out to people who in general didn't care about their own safety was probably not the brightest idea Russell ever had and for all that was about to happen I was to hold him personally responsible.

Two jugs of the rocket fuel later someone had the bright idea of racing horses up a mountain. I'm not sure who had that idea, there have been several culprits suggested, but no one charged with the crime as of yet.

Now a horse race up a mountain while loaded up on moonshine would be a wild enough idea for most people, but we added the condition that it should be bareback. Again, I have no idea who made the suggestion it just happened that way.

We agreed on a trail which was more, or less, a mile straight up the side of a mountain and off we set.

The horses we rode were a mixed bag. I was on Indy, a former flat track runner who was at the Haynes' farm to be either sold as a stallion or turned into a steeplechase horse; given his serious lack of interest in mares it looked like jumping was going to be in his future. Russell rode Shady Valley, a horse who had won flat, hurdle and timber races, as well as a horse who was still running well at ten-years-old. Bruce, David, Vann and Will rode steeplechase horses whose names escape me.

Bruce took the early lead and I was happy to sit just off his shoulder thinking I could pass him whenever I felt the time was right. I could hear yelling in behind me as Russell was trying some NASCAR moves on Will by running him into trees as a way to stop him from passing everyone else.

We flew up this thing, and as we were closing in on the finish, I realized Bruce had no intention of losing and for some reason my horse was content to let him stay ahead. Sure enough, Bruce won and the rest of us left in the race banged around as we fought to finish second, which Russell ended up taking.

We got back to the barn in pretty good spirits. Bruce had won with a cagey ride, and Russell had tried to drop the rest of us with his version of NASCAR style horse racing.

In the days, weeks, and months that followed, everyone remembered the ride for the pure fun that it was. As for my part, I remembered the ride for the sheer joy I saw shared between a father and his sons. The race also reminded me of the relationship I wanted with my boys and left me wondering if I would ever get to that point in life with them.

I also remembered that moonshine-induced race up that mountain because a few weeks later Bruce suddenly passed away. He was out feeding his horses one morning and suffered a massive heart attack. It was over rather quickly, but I admired the fact that he went out doing what he loved most.

In the time after his father's death, Russell rode in steeplechase races and later became a bloodstock agent. He liked the travel and action involved with selling horses and going to all the various sales. He even had "The Legacy Continues" printed on his cards. He learned a lot from his dad and probably the most important thing his dad taught him was honesty.

One day when Russell was in Maryland checking out a few horses, I met up with him at Timonium, where

I was riding. Russell looked me over and said, "You're looking rough, man."

I knew he was right. I hadn't gotten to the point where I liked myself, but I was trying.

We went to dinner where Russell told me that he would be back in October for the yearling sales. He invited me to come along and help him go over some prospects. I gladly accepted.

A few days before I was supposed to meet Russell, I took a heavy fall working a horse at Bowie and broke a few ribs so taking a few easy days at the sales was a welcome relief.

We walked around looking at all the horses. Maybe the next Kentucky Derby winner would be hiding among the five hundred or so yearlings we were looking at.

It was fun to think about the possibilities, but also hard, as I knew that for a large number of them there wouldn't be a garland of roses, but a daily grind around a small race track running for their feed.

I knew it all to well.

While at the sales, we paid special attention to the horses' confirmations and pedigrees. We sought out the ones who looked great, but maybe had a weak pedigree, all in the hope of getting them at bargain prices.

The funny thing is that even though I wasn't in the market to buy a prospect, I managed to find a great bargain and a winner, but it wasn't the type you might expect.

Russell wanted to look at fifty or so horses in one particular consignment and as we rounded the corner of the barn where the horses were stabled I slowed down as Russell kept going. I recognized the girl running the place. It was Krissy. It had been at least ten years since we'd gone our separate ways.

She looked the same, maybe better. I looked at her and instantly thought about how life would've been had I just taken a chance.

I walked away and texted Russell saying my ribs were sore and I would meet him inside the sales pavilion whenever he was done looking.

In reality, I was running away from Krissy. I didn't know what I would say to her, and I knew I looked like I'd just walked out of a concentration camp; besides, it wasn't easy for me to face someone I'd hurt.

When I met up with Russell later, I told him the story about Krissy and how I'd chased her away. He laughed and called me a "chicken," but for some reason he knew I was serious about wanting to talk to her.

We decided to go back so he could have another look at a horse and this time I would go in with him. The plan was to play it smooth and not say much just let her know I was around.

It was a great plan until I realized she really didn't recognize me! If I was going to get her to notice me I was going to have to actually talk to her.

Mustering up all the courage I could, I walked up to Krissy and said hello. She didn't turn a cold shoulder so right off the bat I felt like maybe she'd forgiven me, or at the very least forgotten about our first time around. We did the usual how have you been routine and that was pretty much that. I didn't ask for her number as it just didn't seem like the thing to do and to be honest I was afraid she would turn me down.

By the time Russell and I decided to head home it was getting dark. In order to get back to the parking lot, we had to walk past the barn where Krissy was working.

I've always been "ballsy" on the track and believed that you made your own way if you have the courage; that's to say that it bothered me that I hadn't asked Krissy for her number.

As luck would have it, as we were walking, I noticed that Krissy was having trouble getting one of her horses loaded on a trailer.

I volunteered Russell for the mission, while Krissy, my broken ribs and I lent him serious moral support.

After the horse was loaded Krissy, and I talked a little and I asked her for her number and even for a date. She was pretty hesitant, but I convinced her by saying,

"What's the worst that can happen? You get a free meal and with luck, you will at least leave thinking I'm less of an asshole than when you walked in."

For some reason my way of thinking worked. We went out and in the following weeks continued to see each other. Eventually, Krissy asked me to come up to her place so we could go trail riding. I really wasn't sure about the idea. I mean, I ride horses every day so going out to ride a horse on a day off seemed like work.

I got to Krissy's place and as we prepared to go for our ride, she asked, "You don't need a saddle do you?"

I really didn't know what to say. "Ahh not really I suppose, I should be fine." I felt good about my response, especially since there was no moonshine involved.

My mount, Dylan, was a paint pony that looked like he had never missed a meal in his life. He was like riding an armchair with legs, but I could tell by his eyes that he was a gentle horse.

Krissy and I rode for an hour or more. Watching her, I could see the joy I was missing. I realized, yet again, that I needed a serious break from racing. I needed time to let my body and mind heal, but, like I said before, I needed to keep riding in order to provide for my boys.

Krissy and I started seeing each other pretty much everyday. Onc again, we just seemed to fit and despite the fact that I was riding when I should've been on a beach on the Bahamas getting my head together with Krissy by my side, I found that I was happy; as happy as I'd been in very, very long time.

During the time that I started seeing Krissy on a steady basis, I was riding at the Timonium races. On one particular day, I saw a poster advertising the fact that Walt Disney Studios was looking for riders to take part in a movie they were filming based on the life of Triple Crown winner Secretariat.

As you know, I've always been adventurous so I called thinking it would be a neat little story for the future, to say I was in a movie. Besides, phone calls had always had a way of changing my life so I thought what the heck, I'll give it a try.

I called and left a message on one of those voicemail collection things where you get the recording and are told to leave a message and a consultant will return your call. I left my details and never gave the matter a second thought.

Being in a movie was a nice idea, but reality suggested that there was no way that they would ever return my call.

Now, I don't know what it is about me and phone calls, but on one night as I was leaving Penn National after winning a race for Wendy Kinnamon on a real quirky filly called Sack of Rubies, I received a call from Shannon Cain, a representative for the movie. She asked if I was Tom Foley.

I think I said, "Yes, I'm Tom Foley," but I really don't remember.

"Good," she answered, "we got your message. Is there any chance you could be in Lexington, Kentucky, on Friday morning by eleven?"

Lexington? Hell, I would've driven to Tibet for a shot at being in a movie.

Shannon told me where to be and who to see and that was pretty much it. I was already booked to ride that Thursday night at Charlestown so it was going to be a drive all night to reach Lexington in time. You drive so much as a jockey that the nine hours in a car are really not all that daunting.

I rode my horses that night at Charlestown and set off for Kentucky at midnight. There was no point in trying to catch a few hours of sleep as I was wired from the races and had that whole little kid at Christmas feeling going on.

Reaching Kentucky, I stopped at an IHOP and ate a big breakfast.

I got rid of it right away.

With nothing else to do, I drove to the address I was given and checked in.

I went in and met the casting director. She was setting up all her cameras and jotting down some notes. She looked at me kind of puzzled and asked if I was there to read and if I had my "sides."

To be honest, I really didn't know what I was there for. I told her that I was asked to show up and that I knew I was early, but thought it best to go ahead and check in.

She marked me down as reading for the part of Ron Turcotte, Secretariat's go-to jockey. She then gave me the sides, which I learned right there and then were what they called pages with the lines from a movie written on them. She told me to read them over and then to come back, and she would film me playing out the part.

It sounded pretty simple; four lines and away you go. At least, that's what I thought.

Not a chance, I couldn't remember my lines and was really nervous about the whole thing. To call it a disaster would be fair. She said that I was not really the description for Turcotte, but she thought I would suit the role of Jimmy Gaffney, Secretariat's exercise rider.

She asked if I could come back for a one o'clock meeting with her and her production assistant.

I knew I was horrible at the first audition and really the only reason I thought she wanted me to come back was because she liked the Irish flat hat that I was wearing. Besides, at this point I thought Gaffney was Irish so it all seemed to make sense, at least for the time being.

Inbetween auditions, I ate lunch at an all-you-can-eat-buffet and flipped before I walked out.

The fact of the matter was that I was an addict and an addict can't stop; when the urges and cravings call, all you can do is answer.

This time around, I only had a couple of lines so I wasn't as nervous. I rattled them off and for some reason I thought it was best to act like I was on a horse as that's where, according to the sides, I was meant to be speaking from.

When I was done, I petted my make-believe Secretariat and they liked it. There was only one problem, they asked if I could do it all again, and this time with an American accent.

Yes, this was the point where I learned Jimmy Gaffney was an American.

I did my version of an American accent. (I found the fact that I'd heard thousands of Americans butcher my accent and here I was murdering theirs ironic.) The casting director asked if I could come back at seven to meet Mr. Wallace, the movie's director. I said that would be fine and she recommended that I work on my American accent until then.

I agreed.

Off I went and for the rest of the day I talked to myself using my new "American twang". Mr. Wallace turned out to be Randall Wallace of *Braveheart* fame. He was really down to earth. I read the lines for him in my own accent and an American accent. We had a little chat about Ireland and how he loved it there during the filming of *Braveheart*. I wasn't sure how the audition went, but was happy with the fact that I'd gotten a chance to chat with him. He seemed really interested in the things we were talking about.

I didn't get the "don't call us, we'll call you" line it was just the "thanks and we'll be in touch" line, which I took as the "thanks for trying" line.

Miracles of miracles, two days later I was offered the part of Jimmy Gaffney. I was over the moon with the news. My friends got wind of it and were joking that I would come back from Hollywood a changed person.

They were right, just not in the way they figured.

Inbetween the time that I landed the role of Jimmy Gaffney and the time that I was scheduled to begin filming in Louisiana, Krissy and I kept seeing each other on a regular basis. I was still flipping, but I tried to stop as my date to leave drew closer.

I thought that they would notice the little cracks on the corners of my lips from where my fingers would rub or that my eyes were bloodshot or that my voice would be different from the acid burning my throat.

It was hard to stop, especially since I was still playing the game. I knew that riding was my job and that this role would provide me with a distraction for a few weeks, but as soon as it was over, I knew that bulimia was there waiting for me.

Bulimia lived in my head; it was always talking to me. If I ate something and felt like I didn't get it all up, I would just eat again and drink more soda and then tried again to root it all out.

My first real shock on the set occurred when I discovered that we were supposed to put on our costume when we showed up and into makeup right afterwards. I'd never worn makeup so while the makeup crew was putting the stuff on me, I wondered aloud how I was going to eat with it on. They told me not to worry, just to eat, and then one of them jokingly added that I shouldn't cry. It was funny, but as I noted earlier, there's always tears when you flip.

The second thing that surprised me on the set was when I found out that they really do feed everybody well when making a movie.

I was confused. I knew I couldn't just go sit there and not eat and now because I was wearing all this makeup I couldn't flip.

Not sure of what to do, I called my dad. He knew about the things I was doing to myself. Time and again he'd made it clear that he didn't approve, but he was always supportive and ready to listen.

After explaining the situation to my dad, he asked me what was the point of being there with the chance to meet and hang out with these people if all I was going to do was sit in my trailer being miserable. He told me that someday I would look back and regret not being a part of it. "Go eat," he said, "take it all in. A few days won't kill you."

Dad was right. I knew that someday I would look back and feel like an idiot for missing out on the experience, but I also knew how much not flipping would kill my weight. "Fuck it," I said, and I went out and joined in.

Diane Lane and John Malkovich were seated at a table and as luck would have it, I got to sit down beside John. I met both of them and the funny thing about it was that John was more familiar with steeplechasing than flat racing so we had a lot to chat about.

Really, it was good to go to the meal because I had a chance to meet John. My first scenes were just with him, so this gave me a chance to talk to him like a regular person. But what really struck me about the meal was that afterwards I felt as if something had changed inside of me. The food felt like a drug that I'd deprived my body, and once "injected" it left me with a renewed energy.

My reaction to the food was one I hadn't expected. On the next day, I ate like a king and kept it all. I was feeling great, but deep inside I knew that as soon as I returned to the real world, I would be right back to flipping.

*M*y role in the movie involved riding "Secretariat" in his morning workouts and talking with the owners and trainers about how he was doing. Pretty much like I'd done on a daily basis for years in the real world.

When we were preparing to film Secretariat's first real fast breeze, Randall Wallace came over and placed his arm around my shoulder. He showed me where the cameras were located, including the one placed near the track; I was suppose to ride Secretariat past this particular camera, and at a good pace.

Mr. Wallace told me not to worry about anything, to have fun. "The light is going fast," he said, "so try to get the horse as close as you can to the camera, but if it can't be done don't worry; we can get it tomorrow. I don't want to over work these horses. If they have a fast gallop I like for them to have a few hours rest before we even think about using them again."

Listening to him, I immediately thought, "Is this guy for real?"

I mean, I couldn't understand how, or why, a person in his position; with all he had going on, was worried about overworking horses.

We shot my scene and everything worked out fine. As soon as I dismounted, Mr. Wallace was the first to instruct someone to take care of the horse. Once again,

I was struck by how much thought he gave to the equine actors.

The funny thing is that it wasn't until later that night that it hit me; it wasn't him that was strange, it was me. From the kid who had loved horses to the man I was now; I'd become another silent witness to the treatment of horses.

The realization was enough to make me sick to my stomach. How had this happened? How had I reached this point in my life?

I thought back to that warrior in Charlestown and realized that it was time for a change, and it couldn't wait another day.

I've always said I preferred horses to people because they are not malicious and won't go out of their way to hurt you. I'd hurt them and myself and now I realized I no longer wanted to be a silent witness to their destruction.

More importantly, I realized that I could no longer keep playing the game.

*M*y body and mind were finally on the same playing field and even if I didn't know how or where to start, I knew I had to begin somewhere, somehow.

I guess it sometimes takes a trip to fantasyland to open your eyes to your own reality.

*A*t the New Holland Horse Auction.

10

The Calling

As I drove home from Louisiana, I thought about all the events that had caused me to question my life and the paths I'd chosen to follow and realized that the time had come to give up my life as a jockey, at least for a while.

I reflected on how I could go about paying my bills and sending my boys money.

I'm not sure why I'd forgotten about it, but as I thought about what to do, Vladimir Cerin, the trainer I had met in California, came to mind. I remembered what he said about how people with talent would always find their place and calling if they were not afraid to look.

It suddenly dawned on me that I could probably find a job training horses. I'm not sure why the idea had never occurred to me since I'd parted ways with my ex-wife. I guess I'd been too focused on riding and winning to give it a second thought. I'm sure Vladimir had thought about it and that he respected me enough as a man that he didn't come out and say it.

I shook my head and smiled. I supppose I'd finally realized that winning is not always defined by finishing first past the post.

When I arrived home, I immediately quit riding.

In the weeks that followed, Krissy and I kept seeing each other. I stayed over at her farm a few nights and soon found myself living with her.

I was lucky; Krissy could've pretty much had any man she wanted, but she was the type of girl that would go to a dog shelter and instead of bringing home the purebred would get the skinny wormy looking runt who needs a bath and a flea collar.

Hey, sometimes you just get lucky.

After moving in with her, I told Krissy about my plan of working with horses. One thing led to another and before I knew it, we had landed a few prospects and were training them together.

The funny thing about it is that prior to meeting up with Krissy, I'd planned on a trip to Patagonia where I was just going to ride along the coast in an effort to rediscover the passion I had for racing and horses when I was a kid. These plans changed after I started working with Krissy. I realized that I didn't need to go to the far side of the world to rediscover my passion because the answer I was looking for was right in my own backyard.

Working with Krissy, I discovered that I was at my happiest while carrying water buckets from the house to the barn when the pipes were frozen, or working with troubled horses that others had written off.

In time, I also realized that I was a lot like a race horse. Race horses need someone to believe in them and be willing to take a chance on them. For me that someone was Krissy; she believed in me, and she was willing to take a chance... another chance, on me.

I don't mean to make it sound like a fairytale, especially in relation to me. I still had problems; when an alcoholic stops drinking, he is still an alcoholic and just because you stop riding races doesn't mean you stop flipping or abusing yourself. For me, there was no off and on switch. I was a flipper and that's it. I would look at my fingers and see the swelling from actually digesting food or maybe my watch seemed tight; there were a lot of different things that pointed to the fact that I was gaining weight. Simply put, the voice inside my head kept telling me that I was fat and that I needed to get rid of the food I was eating.

Krissy knew from years ago that I was a flipper. I was glad she knew because I didn't have to hide my lifestyle from her. She understood what I was going through and how it affected me.

On one particular night, when I was beating down demons, she looked me in the eyes and said, "Tom, you're hard to be around when you're like that. I never said it years ago because I didn't know how to say it, but you're not going to like yourself or fix your relationship with your kids if you're dead."

Krissy was right, and I knew it, but through it all, I was lucky in that she never judged me; she just helped me every step along the way.

Try as hard as I could, there were still times when I felt like I'd eaten too much and could just go and pull the trigger and relieve the pressure. I didn't do it, but believe me I thought about it.

As for the sleeping pills, they were much easier to put down, especially since I wasn't trying to keep from eating and besides a long day's work on Krissy's farm seemed to cure what I was looking for in that department. Of course, it didn't hurt that I was happy.

While I continued working on getting over my eating disorder, I managed to gain weight and I felt better about myself. So much so that I started turning my attention to the plight of retired Thoroughbreds. I'd seen pictures of the kill pens on Facebook and other sites, and it sickened me. The mass of animals that were being cast away and destroyed was awful, but what really got me were the stories of ex-race horses like Ferdinand.

Thoroughbred horse rescuer Diana McClure once told me that she thought putting horses to sleep was a much better option than letting them go through the ordeal of the sale and the meat truck ride, where they are crammed into trucks like chickens, as every pound of flesh counts as a profit to these pirates.

On one particular Monday, Krissy and I traveled to the New Holland Horse Auction, a public sale nicknamed the "New Holland Killer Sale." The auction is the largest of its kind east of the Mississippi.

The sale takes place every Monday and of the approximate two hundred and fifty horses sold, lecherous buyers purchase twenty-five to forty percent of them. On average, they pay no more than a couple of hundred dollars a head and then load their haul on a van and drive them away to the slaughterhouse.

Even though it is illegal for race horses to come straight from the tracks to these auctions, it happens.

When trainers or owners are questioned about them, the usual excuse is, "well, we don't know how many hands they went through before they got there."

Yes, the equine industry warns trainers or owners not to do this, but that's all it is, tough talk, words designed to cover their asses.

The first thing that struck me about New Holland was the smell and the sight of goats, sheep, cows and horses, all crammed into tight little pens.

I hadn't quite gotten a clear understanding of what Diana was talking about, now I knew she was right; a peaceful and controlled end was so much better than a trip to hell on earth; I've got no other words to describe the scene, maybe no writer has, hell on earth it is.

At times like these, it was hard to understand what the horses were thinking. People say, "Oh, they're just dumb animals," but I can tell you firsthand that I've ridden horses who are far more clever than the people who train them and I've seen horses do amazing things in races, so amazing that to call them dumb, would be, well, dumb.

Horses feel pain and fear; they know when they, win, and they get cocky. It's easy to walk down a shedrow at any track and pick out happy horses from depressed ones and if you bother to look, you will see the expressions we see in people; expressions that can tell you what's going on in their heads.

I'd heard from people that New Holland was a sad place, but to see it in the flesh was such a sickening experience; most of these animals were so under weight that if the Society for the Prevention of Cruelty to Animals were there, they would have shut the place down. I mean, even if an animal is destined for slaughter there should be some standards.

Krissy and I walked along the rows and rows of horses and every now and then we would see a really good looking pony or healthy horse. We wondered by what twist of fate or bad luck, had these healthy horses ended up here.

You just don't know; a divorce, a bad financial move, a foreclosure. It's probably not really a surprise with our current economic situation to see this. Perhaps the owners that sold them in the first place thought that they were selling their horses to people they thought were going to provide them with good homes, but instead ended up here rolling the dice.

If horses are lucky someone will see their potential and buy them to ride, and if they're not lucky some transport pirate will see their meat value and snap them up and send them on their way to slaughter.

As Krissy and I were walking around, she suddenly pointed to a horse standing in a line with other horses bought by the killers. "I know that horse," she said as she held my hand and we walked over to him.

"I think I know him," she said quietly, "we sold him as a two-year-old through a place where I worked. He went for ninety thousand dollars. I just know it's him."

Krissy ran her hands over the big chestnut and looked at the markings all over his body. We looked under his lip and read off his tattoo number. He wasn't that old so the tattoo was very clear. (All race horses must be tattooed before they can run, sometimes when horses have similar markings it's the only way to make sure the right horse is running in the right race.)

"It's Body Rock," Krissy said as she patted his neck. "I just know that it's him."

Some ladies who go around to these sales looking for race horses to rescue were standing nearby. They overheard Krissy. One of them volunteered to call a friend in order to verify if this was Body Rock. She made the call and sure enough, this horse was him.

Krissy was right, Body Rock *had* sold for ninety thousand dollars. As a two-year-old, he had won one hundred and twenty-five thousand dollars before slipping down the ladder.

It happens every day, fast horses like Body Rock stop responding to drugs or needles to block the pain of injury so they are dropped down in claiming price in the hope that someone will take them and their problems with them.

So here Body Rock stood tied to a rail; a ninety-thousand dollar horse that had done his job well on the track was waiting to go off to slaughter after being bought by the transport pirate for the grand sum of two-hundred dollars.

I could tell by the looks in the horses' eyes that they knew their fate. I could see the fear and confusion, but not Body Rock. He had a kind look to him. His big eyes just seemed so gentle and questioning. He might not have remembered Krissy, but given his position, I think he was just glad to see a caring face.

How had this happened?

All I can say is that Body Rock had run three months before he was standing here tied to the rail. He ran poorly and had just one published work a few weeks after that race. Yet here he now stood, three-hundred pounds underweight with the same shoes he had raced in still on three of his feet. (Race horses run in special shoes that are lightweight, so tell me, how many hands had he been through before he ended up here?)

Calls were made and some girls who lived about an hour from the sale volunteered to take Body Rock.

The girls found the transport pirate and asked about buying him. He said he would sell them the horse, but not for at least double what he had just paid for him.

Now, he knew these girls didn't have much money, but he also knew they were not leaving without the horse. He'd played this game long enough to know that emotions run deep on the side of saving a horse from slaughter. He knew exactly how to manipulate these kids and he did; the price for saving Body Rock was four hundred and seventy-five dollars.

Once the price was paid, the transport pirate told the girls not to say a word to management as it was against the rules.

Maybe calling him a pirate was too kind, as at least some pirates are compassionate and have a flair about them; this man had neither. He saw nothing wrong with what he was doing; he was another happy shylock dealing in pounds of flesh.

Body Rock was saved, but the sad part is that there are dozens of sales and each one will have dozens of Body Rocks; horses who faithfully served their masters, only to be forgotten and sent to slaughter.

Leaving New Holland that day, I realized that I would never be able to turn my back on these horses.

I thought about the warrior who had broken his knee at Charlestown. I was relieved that he had been hurt bad enough to be destroyed there and then, because if I had found out later that he had ended up in a place like this after saving my life, I don't think I could've gone on living with myself.

The Tom of old, like the one who had ridden in Japan, wouldn't have given these horses a second thought, but the Tom I was becoming would never turn his back on these horses; not as a trainer, an owner, and perhaps someday as a jockey.

*M*e and Krissy. Yes, sometimes the runt
of the litter gets lucky.

11

The Simple Game

As I'm finishing this book, I'm back to my normal weight of one hundred and forty-five pounds. I'm still living with Krissy, and we're still training horses together. I see my boys more often as it's easier to visit them now that I'm not worried about my weight. Every now and then, I'm dad, but mostly it's Tom. Rome wasn't built in a day; that's to say that maybe in time I will have the relationship with them that Bruce enjoyed with his boys. When that happens, it will be the biggest win in my life.

The urge to flip lives with me on a daily basis; I guess it always will. But, you know, that kid that grew up in Ireland wanting nothing more in life than to be a jockey also lives with me on a daily basis, and I guess he always will too.

When I'm alone and I think back on that kid, I always smile when I'm reminded of just how simple he saw the game.

In the end, I guess he had it right; the game *is* simple; as simple as you're willing to make it.

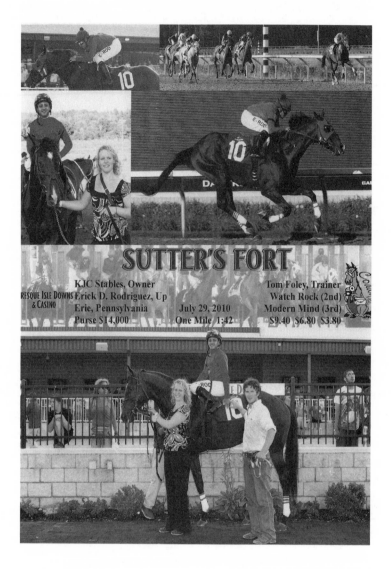

SUTTER'S FORT

KJC Stables, Owner		Tom Foley, Trainer
PRESQUE ISLE DOWNS & CASINO	Erick D. Rodriguez, Up	Watch Rock (2nd)
	Erie, Pennsylvania	July 29, 2010	Modern Mind (3rd)
	Purse $14,000	One Mile 1:42	$9.40 $6.80 $3.80

*P*osing proudly in the winner's circle
as the trainer of Sutter's Fort.

Acknowledgements

Aside from those mentioned in the book, I would like to acknowledge the following people: Barry Batterton, Beertruck, Jean Baum, Charlie and Happy Chandler, Jim Culletton, Jimmy Duggan, Steve Duggan, Craig Faine, Holly Ferris, Karen Gray, David Hackett, Simon Hobson, Gustavo Larrosa, Frank Lyons, Mark McEntee, Mark Madden, Ann Majette, Anthony Mawing, Darren Nagle, Jonathan Sheppard, Cameron Walker, Tim Walsh, Timmy Wyatt, Chris Young, and everyone else who has helped and guided me along the way.